W9-BRJ-025

THE GRAND EXPERIMENT

THE GRAND EXPERIMENT

An Expedition of Self-Discovery

MADREN CAMPBELL
GAYLE GREGORY
KAREN JOHNSON

PURE POSSIBILITY

Copyright © 2006 by Madren Campbell, Gayle Gregory
and Karen Johnson

All rights reserved. No part of this book may be
reproduced or transmitted in any form or by any means,
electronic or mechanical, including photocopying,
recording, or by any information storage and retrieval
system without permission in writing from the publisher.

Library of Congress
Catalog Card Number: 2006933316

ISBN: 978-0-9789191-0-8

Published by Pure Possibility, LLC
2121 Reed Rd., Hood River, Oregon 97031

Printed and bound in the United States of America on acid
free paper.

Bless the preciousness of this moment
that brings us to the possibility
of seeing through mind's devices and
opening to our heart's pure design.

CONTENTS

ACKNOWLEDGMENTS

With gratitude to our dear friends and guinea pigs, Char Edwards, Terri Orloff, Colleen Rugh and Christine Toscano, who gave us such great feedback and support in the early stages of our project. A gracious thank you also to Dr. Suzanne McConnell, who took our first fledgling draft and returned it to us with advice, suggestions and feedback that we integrated into what became our first real draft. She taught us a great deal with her critical eye. Suzanne, a professor at Rutgers and an editor and author herself, took the time out of her busy schedule to help us in our process and we will be forever grateful. We would also like to express our awe of Judiann White, who discovered the link between our myths and the chakras. Her insight into the connection added a dimension that took the book to a new level of depth. Lastly, we would like to thank Michael Friend, of Inei-Re Retreat Center, who was immensely helpful during the final edits of our book.

We would like to honor and acknowledge two awe-inspiring teachers, Elle Collier Re (Inei-Re) and Aja Thomas (Atma Institute). We are who we are today because of their clarity and unconditional love. No words could capture our gratitude and appreciation. They are always in our hearts.

We bow humbly before our life partners, Ken Gregory, John Brookshier and Joy Kanevski, whose support, encouragement and inspiration graced this project. They are our heroes and coaches and we are forever grateful for their love, caring and willingness to share and live, fully engaged in this amazing grand experiment.

We have great reverence for all the people and places that have touched our lives and deepened our life experience—thank you for all the lessons—every one of them. Everything that has happened up to this point and everything that will happen from this point forward has but one purpose, to open our hearts, our minds and our spirits to the possibility of being One.

SET UP TO WIN

Careful observation and attention will be indispensable in order to fully connect with the opportunity presented by *The Grand Experiment.* We recommend the use of a simple journal to capture insights and growing awareness as you begin to integrate the material from the book into your life. If possible, enlist the help of a mentor to walk with you. A human reminder of your commitment is often beneficial, as any time we enter into communion with another we summon assistance beyond our ordinary understanding.

This book is about confronting everything you've put together to survive, so don't be surprised if you have strong reactions to the journey upon which you are embarking. In fact, expect to feel confronted. Expect resistance. Expect your emotions to feel assaulted at times. Also expect to feel your heart open. Expect to see glimpses into the truth of who you really are. Expect to watch as old beliefs splinter and begin to fall away. When you open to being honest, which this process requires, anything you are avoiding, ignoring, denying, suppressing, or coping with—basically everything that is not healed—will come up to be completed in one form or another. See this as a gateway to the road less traveled and you may just find that which is central to living life in full authenticity.

To find the gift in what arises requires discipline. If you find yourself blaming another and projecting your feelings onto someone other than yourself, if you find yourself bored, disinterested, or thinking you've already heard, done or know this, if you find yourself wanting to move quickly through one section or another, if you find yourself stuck, unable to move forward, if you find yourself emotional—angry, sad, resentful—know that you and the book are getting the job done. You are uncovering those things you have been prideful about, avoiding, resisting, or unwilling to look at in your life. Look deeply into your projection, your boredom, your knowing, your impatience, your particular emotion and find the pure message within its outer covering.

The book provides tools to expose your myths—the belief systems that determine your life, the limits you put on yourself and others that determine your behavior and create your reality. You provide the discipline to do the lessons. With introspection and reflection you bring the light of awareness to the words and make them real. The lessons are important. It is through them that you have the opportunity to experience the Truth at a cellular level rather than as intellectual curiosity. Trust the process and the design. By working through the lessons, you will learn to trust your own listening. We promise that if you practice the lessons your authentic nature will begin to unfold.

We know what we are asking you to do. We have done,

and continue to do this work. We know how scary and painful it can be. We are asking you to stay present to the fear, knowing that none of us like the darkness. When we wrote the book we had to be present with our own fears or we couldn't move forward. Each time we resisted, in one form or another, the book stopped. Through the process we began to trust that when we see negative emotions coming up they are a gift from Source. Negative emotions are pointers— they tell us 'stop!' there is something here of importance; this is the time to look within.

Ideally the book is designed to be read front to back, with time taken for introspection at each pre-planned step along the way. Each chapter has associated lessons that have been designed as an integral part of the book. They build on each other, as does the book from chapter to chapter, to allow an increased depth and opening of awareness to occur. As we have practiced the lessons ourselves, we have found the full spectrum of feelings, emotions, reactions, thoughts and physical sensations arising.

Give yourself permission to take the time necessary to care for yourself as you practice these lessons. This is a healing process. As with most healing processes, there will be toxins, in one form or another, released. Be kind to yourself—your mind, body and spirit—throughout the process.

STOP, LOOK AND LISTEN

STOP, LOOK AND LISTEN is a three-step tool that will help you see your thoughts as they appear. It is foundational for all the lessons in the book. This is a simple but profound process to use as you start on your journey down the path to your authentic self. At first you will use it to see how fear shows up, the masks it wears, in your daily life. As you feel stuck, overwhelmed or out of balance, return to it again and again to re-center yourself and to move through resistance. As you peel away the layers of belief this tool can become seamlessly integrated and a natural extension of awareness.

STOP—Bring your awareness to the moment. The point of stopping is just to stop. Don't worry about when. It doesn't have to look like anything specific. There is no correct way. Stop:
- ☐ Take a deep breath
- ☐ Call a mental time out

LOOK—Become the observer. See your thoughts in a big picture window. See them move across your view. Don't hang onto them. Don't take them for a ride. Just watch them go by.
Look at:
- ☐ Thoughts
- ☐ Reactions
- ☐ Decisions

Notice:
- ☐ Where does this thought come from?
- ☐ Am I generating this thought?
- ☐ Does this thought determine my behavior?
- ☐ Do I need to act on my thought?
- ☐ Is this thought based in fear?

LISTEN—Listen to what you do with the thoughts. Listen to how your body reacts. If one thought hooks you and you take it for a ride, be aware that you have done that and go back to the picture window. If you hear a thought, say to yourself, "Oh! There's a thought," and return to your role as the observer of the thoughts in the picture window without analyzing further.

Listen:

- ☐ Pay attention to the thought that hooks you
- ☐ Acknowledge the thought
- ☐ Return to the picture window
- ☐ Listen to see if you are judging yourself for having the thought
- ☐ See the judgment as a thought that has hooked you
- ☐ Begin the process again

The initial purpose of this tool is to begin identifying for yourself, the constant dialog that is going on in your head, and to start discovering that who you are may be something different than this constant comment. This dialog is your road map to your thoughts and beliefs—your current wiring. At this moment you may be thinking, "Dialog, there is no dialog in my head. What are you talking about?" THAT'S the dialog we are talking about.

Choose to have fun with this. Life doesn't have to be so serious. In fact, our seriousness tells us that we are protecting and defending our sense of self. Loosen your grip a bit and slip into a whole new way of being.

THE GRAND EXPERIMENT

1
PATH TO DISCOVERY

At some point in our lives, if we are lucky, it dawns on us that something is missing. No matter how successful we are in terms of the material things we have attained, we know there is something more. And if we're truly blessed, we begin to look beyond those things we have reached for in the past and thus the journey begins.

The Grand Experiment is a path to the discovery of our authentic selves. It invites us to uncover our myths, the beliefs that we have unconsciously embraced as our reality, and asks us to reexamine their validity. It challenges us to face the very fears that have created the longing in our hearts. It opens the door to the possibility that what we are searching for is unconditional love and it is only our fear that has obscured our view.

When we aren't feeling safe and good about ourselves and life isn't going the way we want it to and think it should, we can count on one thing—fear is in the picture. Fear is so pervasive and ingrained in our every day lives that we don't recognize it; we don't even see that it is there. In fact, usually we call it by another name.

It shows up in the body as tightness in our chest, maybe in our throat, maybe in our gut. Each one of us is different. If we stop to think about it, each of us knows where it hides. It's the constipation, the diarrhea, the headache, and the inability to get it up and keep it up. It's the extra pounds that we can't seem to get rid of. It's the allergies and hair loss. It's pain. It's suffering.

Outwardly it sounds like, "It's all your fault. . .I have a headache. . .I'm too stressed. . .I'm just so tired. . .I hate this . . .I can't deal with this anymore. . .GAWD! I need something to eat." Inwardly, the chatter might sound like, "Who do you think you are. . .you don't know anything. . .how dare you treat me this way." And if you dig a little deeper, you might hear, "There is no way this is going to work. . .what will people think of me. . .I'm not good enough. . .who do I think I am. . .boy, I should just play it safe."

Fear looks like not knowing what to do and not having the answer to fix the problem. It's that tight knot in the stomach when faced with being alone—whether it is long term or just being alone for the evening. It's how we feel when we look in the mirror and see the bags under our eyes, the saggy breasts, the rolls of fat, or the strange man or woman looking back at us with regret and longing, wondering what happened to life. That's fear staring back at us. We see it and know it's there in that instant when we feel vulnerable or exposed. That's often the same instant that we slam the door shut and deny fear's existence. It is just too scary.

We generally have a negative judgment about fear. The connotation is that it is bad or wrong. We judge fear as something to be avoided. But, fear is actually a useful tool. It is an instinctual response mechanism, designed to signal when a perceived danger or threat is present. It is an indicator, a barometer, rather than something to be denied or avoided. Fear presents an opportunity for growth and understanding, and when embraced, allows us to continually develop. When we have awareness of the fear, it gives us a choice to move from actions consistent with the fear that usually result in unhappiness and pain, to a way of being that is more in line with our personal commitments and vision of who we want to be.

There is a way out of being solely determined by fear, a way out of the frustration and upset. In order to find it we must be willing to question those beliefs we hold dear and that hold us hostage. We must question the myths, and specifically, the original myth, which is the belief that we are separate from our Source.[1] This is the myth that creates all the myths that we live with and is the root of all our unhappiness. It is such a sacred myth that it goes unquestioned. It's the basic belief, the belief underlying all beliefs, which drives our behaviors and actions. Our willingness to question the myths opens the door to the grand experiment.

---

[1] For the context of this book, what some people call God, Source, Brahman, Allah, Yahweh, Buddha, The Universe, Higher Self, or other names, we use four words interchangeably, Source, Oneness, Wholeness and Love.

LESSON—HEEEERE'S FEAR

Exercise #1

<u>Purpose:</u> To begin to pay attention to the prevalence of fear and how fear presents itself to you externally.

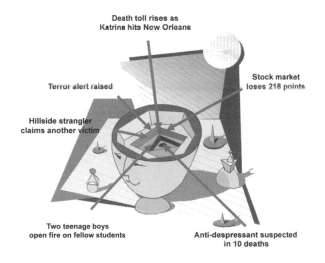

<u>Instructions:</u> Pay attention to the headlines in your local paper, the news and programming that you watch, and what you hear when you are engaged in conversation. As thoughts appear write them down in your journal. Get them out of your head and look at them. Do this exercise for seven days. Ask yourself the following questions:

1. What is it I am hearing?
2. What is it I am seeing?
3. What do I feel?
4. What sensations are happening in my body?

Exercise #2

<u>Purpose:</u> To begin to pay attention to the prevalence of fear and how it presents itself to you internally.

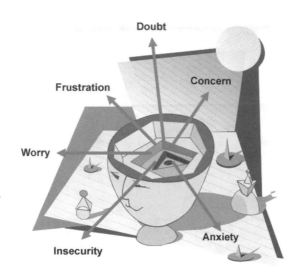

<u>Instructions:</u> Prepare to write down words and phrases describing areas where you may have concern, anxiety, doubt, worry, frustration and insecurity in your life—the strategies that hide your fear. Take twenty minutes and open your mind and break loose the floodgate. It doesn't have to be precise; it doesn't have to be in order. Don't stop to make it neat; don't stop to make complete sentences. Let it flood out as openly and completely as you can.

2
THE POWER OF
OUR BELIEFS

My partner's son woke up in the morning with an allergic reaction—lots of mucous, blowing his nose—in general, feeling miserable. I commented to John, my partner, that perhaps this was a result of the ice cream he ate the night before. He responded that it was due to working outdoors that day and not what he was eating. He said, "That's your belief, not mine." And I retorted, "No, that's science." I realized that I do have very strong beliefs around diet and its impact on our health and not everyone shares my beliefs. Karen J.

Our beliefs are generated from the basic foundation of the myths. They create the context for our lives. They color our experience of life and from this we create our stories about others and ourselves. We think that our beliefs are who we are. They become our identity. We rarely examine them. They become agreements that we make with ourselves. We have beliefs about everything: the best color of skin, how much money we need in savings to be safe, the right way to eat, how green the grass should be, how to be in relationships, which, if any, political party to belong to, the best country to live in, how our loved ones should behave, whether the toilet seat should be up or down, when its safe to speak, the best religion. The list of our beliefs is finite although sometimes seems never ending.

So where do these beliefs come from? Beliefs arise out of thoughts. Thoughts occur as circumstances happen. We react to the circumstances and then after the experience we analyze it and make decisions. Those decisions create our experience of life. These experiences are primarily based in fear, a result of the underlying myths. Fear becomes our conditioned habit through which we view and interpret life, and over time these habits become normal. We are hardwired for stability—to maintain the status quo—to avoid change. Addictions capture our desired sense of the familiar, which then further stabilizes what we see as normal. As thoughts and decisions pile up, we turn them into beliefs. These beliefs automatically determine our behavior and actions.

According to quantum physicists, everything is energy, including us. Thoughts are energy, and we attract thought energy that vibrates at the same frequency we do. Some thoughts just pass through without much notice, obviously incompatible with our frequency. Some stick and are so invasive that we can't shake them, no matter how hard we try, because we resonate with those thoughts. "Oh, that one again!"

We call these thoughts Velcro Thoughts, because even when we make a decision to change something, like becoming more authentic, old familiar thoughts in apparent opposition to our decision, continue to plague us—sticking to us like Velcro. Until we change our resonance by increasing our awareness, the same thoughts will continue to stick.

The power of belief occurs in the 'of the world' domain. This is the domain that we call life and living. This is the domain of the five senses, the domain of our everyday life experience, and also the domain of hopes, dreams, and goals. This is the domain where transformation is a possibility.

Beliefs are what create the fabric of our lives. Until we uncover our beliefs, our lives will continue to be cataleptically, rather than consciously, determined by them.

CATALEPTIC
Catalepsy   Oxford Dictionary American Edition, 1996—A state of trance or seizure with loss of sensation and consciousness accompanied by rigidity of the body. Cataleptic, adj. & noun

CONSCIOUS
Conscious—Oxford Dictionary American Edition, 1996—1. Awake and aware of one's surroundings and identity. 2. Aware; knowing. 3. Realized or recognized by the doer; intentional.

We behave as though we actually are our beliefs, though we don't know this and don't see this most of the time. Our beliefs create our identity: who we perceive our self to be. We live as though our beliefs are having the conversations; our beliefs are reacting; our beliefs are emoting. Our beliefs determine our experience of reality. Our conversations are generated from our beliefs, hidden in the background. We become our beliefs, whatever they may be. Beliefs created from our thoughts and decisions make up the substance of our identity—the myths within which we live. Instead of living fresh in each moment, we live as our identity.

Beliefs don't occur outside of us; we are the ones who choose to create them. Someone suggests something to us and we make a decision to agree with the suggestion or not. As we agree, we may be reinforcing beliefs we already have in place or we may be revising beliefs or creating new ones. It is very, very subtle. The beliefs become our crystalline shell as we invest ourselves in them. The more invested we become in our beliefs, the thicker and harder the shell, which filters and clouds our ability to clearly discern our beliefs. As we integrate beliefs more and more, we become them. We can't even consider giving them up because we don't recognize they exist, so there is nothing to give up. They have become 'us', our reality of the way the world is—or at least the way we believe it should be.

Something's happened to me. I've noticed it within the last six years of surfing. It doesn't occur when I am in the water. It occurs before I go out into the water in certain areas. It's like I have created my own personal red triangle—it extends from just north of Santa Cruz, California all the way through the Pacific Northwest. It is not the water temperature or the wave power or size. It isn't even my fitness level although that does factor into my enjoyment. When I am fit I enjoy it; when I'm not I don't. There is this sense of a man-eating chomper that is going to come up from the depths and have me for lunch. It gets reinforced every time I hear about a shark attack. It started when I saw a great white emerge next to a guy sitting on a longboard, about thirty feet away from me in Northern Oregon. He broke the surface and then just disappeared. I sat there watching the other three surfers paddle in like crazy, having a conversation in my head as to whether that was a sea-lion or a shark. It was odd. I've never seen one since, other than in my dream, but every once in a while I think about it. I haven't surfed the Northwest in six years. Madren C.

THE CRYSTALLINE SHELL

Picture a young child around age three. She is curious about everything, embracing whatever experience comes her way. She is unencumbered by limitation. She is free to choose the direction and interpretation of her life. She has no concepts of picket fences, knights in shining armor, glass ceilings or anything but possibility. Life is joyful. Life is exciting and a wonderment.   She lives in the present moment, occupied totally by what is happening 'right now'.

Picture a teenager encapsulated by a light film of belief that appears as a thin layer of crystalline substance. He is afraid he won't fit in and will be excluded from the group and often suspects that he isn't quite enough anymore, although he isn't sure why or what to do to fix the problem. He has tasted self-doubt—perhaps he failed his driver's test or experienced his first lost love—and yearns for acceptance. He is innocent and still hopeful, still expecting it all to work out. He can see through the crystalline layer clearly and can still be molded by life's possibility. The path is not yet set. He is free to test a variety of experiences outside the boundary of his current beliefs, outside the boundary of the shell, to see where he wants to belong. As long as the risk is not intolerable, the opportunity to explore still outweighs the restriction of his current belief.

Picture a thirty-year old woman encapsulated in a heavier crystalline layer of belief. It is starting to become opaque, although she believes she is still free to choose, not realizing that her beliefs are determining her behavior and choices. The knight in shining armor turned out to be a frog on a mule.

On her 30th birthday she couldn't shut off the alarm on the clock, and the glass ceiling she was so sure she could crack seems impenetrable. The spectrum of choice is narrowing as her current beliefs restrict the choices available to her. Choosing freely would require deviation from patterns and belief structures already in place. It is still possible, although not probable, to penetrate the shell. The odds are stacking up against any meaningful variation from the current direction. Occasionally she loosens up and pops out of the shell to play in the moment. She softens and remembers, "Oh yes, this is who I am," and in the next instant, finds herself on the inside again, longing to hang on to that piece of herself and that soft, playful moment.

Picture a fifty-five year old man encapsulated in a very thick layer of belief; the thickness has made the shell opaque. To the world he is a success. He has the right car, the right house, and the right wife—all the right trappings. His former wives, children and employees may paint a different picture. He came home one day and his children were grown. It has been years since he sat down and had a conversation with them, figuring that he'd do that when he retired. He is oblivious to the cost of his current beliefs and maintains, with righteous indignation, that he is still the captain of his own destiny. He feels he is successful because he has stayed true to his beliefs. Freedom of choice is severely restricted. Life will have great difficulty penetrating the shell he has created with his beliefs and opinions. It is nearly impossible for him to deviate from his current direction. He is robotic in his reactions to life, predictable in every way—event, programmed response, outcome. When he is bored, he tends to go out and buy something new and even with the new stuff, he can't quite figure out why he doesn't feel good about life and about himself. Whatever excitement and spontaneity there is, is in reaction to the new, the bigger, the better. In those moments when he is by himself he knows that no one really, truly knows him. In fact, he is aware that he doesn't know himself anymore. He sees old age approaching and is deathly afraid that he missed out on something that life had to offer.

Picture a seventy-five year old woman whose crystalline shell is very murky and extremely thick. Were it to crack, she would most likely die, for everything she believes herself to be, everything she sees as important, would be gone. The ego would shatter and the human form could not withstand the shock. Life has not been close to this woman for many years. She hasn't seen her children for a long time. They promise to come by and if they do, they stay for what seems like only a few moments—in a hurry to get back to their own lives. The grandkids haven't called and she quit sending birthday cards years before. If she hasn't already lost her husband she fears that she might lose him at any time or may yearn for the freedom that life as a widow might bring. When this thought appears she stuffs it immediately—how could she think that way? Something must be wrong with her. She closed out life years ago and continued to build up the shell with every new righteousness and knowing she collected. The woman's anger at life grows daily. Her body is beginning to break down. The days are too long and only the frequent naps hasten night's approach. Doing everyday things is much more difficult—shopping, dealing with the world's fast pace, driving in traffic. She's not getting around the way she used to. Going to the doctor has become the outing of the day and there is no energy left for anything else. She feels isolated. The television is her only real friend. She is hardened like the shell and unable to see beyond her self-constructed belief system. She doesn't understand why she feels so lost and alone, so totally disconnected from the rest of life. She is ready to die. She is tired and life has let her down. She doesn't realize that the body just wants to join the heart that died years before.

Our unconscious agreement with the myths causes a cataleptic way of life with very predictable results and little possibility of new openings. Standing in the domain of catalepsy, we are the myths. They are who we have become. In this domain, we live our lives determined by our reactions to the circumstances we find our selves in. The majority of us haven't been introduced to the possibility of another way of living, so this is our normal way of life and being.

LESSON—DREAM A LITTLE DREAM

<u>Purpose:</u> To bring awareness to the power your beliefs have in determining your behavior.

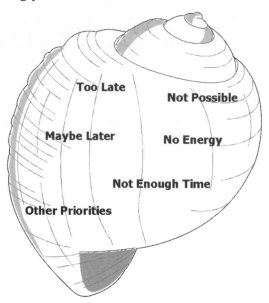

<u>Instructions:</u> Prepare to write your answers to the following questions:

1. What is or was my life's dream?
2. What are my beliefs about my ability to realize my life's dream?
3. What events and resulting beliefs have contributed to the crystallization of my shell?
4. What is the cost of living within the shell?
5. What must I give up to crack my crystalline shell?
6. If I could take away the fear and know that everything in my life would turn out, how would I live my life?

3
THE MOMENT OF AWARENESS—THE EDGE

Call your mind into this sweet stillness—
the sacred spaciousness of awareness.
Elle Collier Re [1]

We will be willing to open to the possibility of the existence of another reality outside the myths, when we recognize that our identity and current way of living is untenable, and doesn't allow us to realize our full potential and never will. It is like coming to grips with life's glass ceiling and discovering that we were the ones who put it there. This is the moment of awareness.

POSSIBILITY
Possibility—*Oxford Dictionary American Edition, 1996*—1. the state or fact of being possible, or an occurrence of this (*outside*

---

[1] More information about Elle Collier Re, an awakened teacher, can be found at Inei-Re.org

the range of possibility; saw no possibility of going away). 2. a thing that may exist or happen *(there are three possibilities).* 3. *(*usu in *pl.)*the capability of being used, improved, etc.; the potential of an object or situation *(*esp. *have possibilities).*

This insight creates the possibility to see the world differently than we currently do. We cannot even glimpse this world, outside the myths, until the possibility is realized. It is physically not available to us. A new reference point is created with the birth of this new possibility.

Without this willingness we will predictably live the life we currently have, in the direction we are currently headed, in the domain of separation. The opportunity that is being presented, is to explore a whole new domain of possibility that we are currently not aware of—it is like trying to suck air through a snorkel, not knowing that if you just lift your head up out of the water and take the snorkel out of your mouth you could inhale freely without pressure and restriction. The possibility of another context is always present whether we are aware of it or not.

I must still be under water!
It couldn't be as easy
as taking the snorkle
out of my mouth....
or could it be?

Recognizing the domain in which we have placed ourselves, we may now be willing to step off the edge and let go of our current reality. When we let go, we create the opportunity to become aware that we are not our identity. That in fact, we are not our thoughts as we previously believed—we have thoughts; additionally, we are not our beliefs—we have beliefs. Thoughts and beliefs only have the power we assign to them. In fact, our thoughts and beliefs have no power until we empower them.

This realization presents the opportunity to change and alter our thoughts and beliefs without losing our sense of who we truly are. All the time and investment we have put into protecting and defending ourselves, thinking that we are our thoughts and beliefs, can now be freed up and redirected to examine our beliefs from a perspective outside of the beliefs, which will allow us to learn and remember our true nature. We then have the opportunity to create a new reality, free of the shackles of the old beliefs.

Thoughts and beliefs are not right or wrong, they are just thoughts and beliefs. Useful questions to ask ourselves are: "Do our current beliefs work for us?" "Are we living our life aligned with who we want to be?" "Do we want to examine only those beliefs that prevent us from having the life we want, or are we open to looking at all our beliefs?" This is an opportunity to examine every one of the beliefs that we have (or that have us). With this examination we can decide whether or not our beliefs are working for us, and then we can replace them if we choose to do so. We also have the opportunity to let them go without replacing them at all. For each individual the answer to these questions will be different

depending on our willingness to go beyond our comfort zone
into uncharted territory.   Depending on our response, Source
will respond in kind, and give us opportunities to examine
and explore those beliefs we are willing to see.

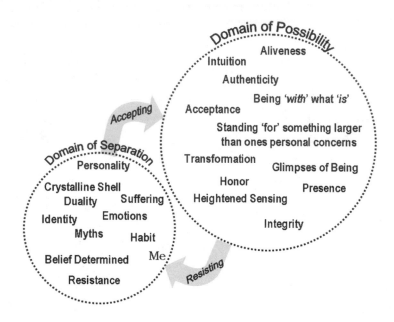

Without this new possibility we will continue to pretend
not to be afraid within the belief of a scary world. We will
continue to search and acquire more, certain that there will
never be enough. We will continue to try to find ways to
control our world within the belief that the power is outside
of ourselves. We will continue to strive for self-acceptance
while knowing that we are not enough. We will continue to
justify and defend our one-right-way, even while knowing
that we may be wrong. We will continue to search for Reality
within the belief that we already know what is real. We will

continue to attempt to find unity within the belief that we are separate and alone.

MOMENT OF CHOICE

We are creating all the time whether cataleptically or consciously. We create by making choices and taking action consistent with those choices. As shown in the following diagram, prior to the moment of awareness we are creating cataleptically—in a trance with loss of sensation and consciousness, accompanied by rigidity of the body. Here we live inside the boundaries of the myths. At the moment of awareness there is a possibility of being unrestricted by the myths. We are standing in the domain of possibility the moment we see another reality exists. It exists as possibility until we make a choice. At the moment of choice we step into the domain of conscious creation.

| Responsibility
Self-expression is:
•Spontaneous
•Animated
We empower those
beliefs consistent with
our commitment | I am aware of my beliefs
I am aware of my thoughts
I am aware of my decisions
I am aware of my reactions
I am aware of my experience
Possibility
Freedom
Choice
CONSCIOUS | I create it
I choose to do it
Authenticity
Accountability
Absolute Control |

———————————————— **Moment of Awareness** ————————————————

| No responsibility
Self-expression is:
•Rigid
•Controlled
We are determined by
our unconscious
beliefs, thoughts, and
decisions | CATALEPTIC
No Choice
No Freedom
Identity
I am my experience
I am my reactions
I am my decisions
I am my thoughts
I am my beliefs | It just happens
I am a victim
Inauthenticity
No accountability
Control is outside |

When we enter the domain of conscious creation we enter the domain of moment-by-moment choice. This is a new reality. The choice will always be to stay or to step out of being determined by the myths. Every moment and every circumstance in life is an opportunity to examine and to choose to see life as an experiment-in-action.

LESSON—UNDER THE MICROSCOPE

<u>Purpose:</u> To examine life as possibility.

<u>Instructions:</u> Prepare to write your answers to the following questions:

1. What fears and beliefs about my self and my life prevent me from being willing to live my life as possibility?

2. Am I willing to let go of those fears and beliefs and create a new reality?

<u>4</u>
EXPERIMENT ESSENTIALS

Scientists set up their laboratory with appropriate tools and equipment to begin all experiments. As we embark upon this process, we are not unlike the scientist. There are distinctive components to the equipment that we require for our grand experiment. Each component is as essential to the fulfillment of the experiment as any other. As we continue with our experiment our list of useful tools and gear may naturally expand along with our awareness.

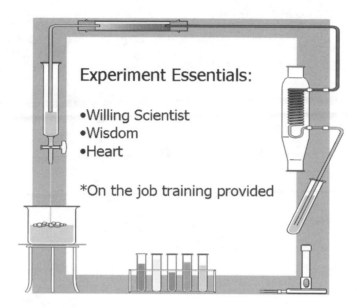

Experiment Essentials:

•Willing Scientist
•Wisdom
•Heart

*On the job training provided

WISDOM

Wisdom lives in awareness. We gain wisdom by learning about ourselves and the world in which we live. We do that by bringing every experience, everything we do and say, into conscious awareness. We learn about ourselves by noticing when we are putting on masks or playing charades. It doesn't matter why we do it—maybe we are scared, maybe we want to make a good impression—but what we do know is that it doesn't feel pure, it doesn't feel whole. We know that it is not who we are. And so to learn about ourselves we learn to notice and be sensitive to all the ways we turn away from our true nature, thinking we are protecting ourselves. As we learn about ourselves and discover how often we pretend, we also discover how it doesn't feel good, and gain the wisdom that we can stop the pretense any time we choose.

As we let go of the need to protect and defend, and choose instead to **LEARN AND GROW,** we learn to not know and to discover. We put on our beginner mind and keep it on for the duration of the experiment. Adventure *is* fun! We can use this as our new mantra. Our willingness to not know, to step into life and be in the presence of the fear and uncertainty and stay true to our hearts allows us to grow and experience our innocence, which is, at the very least, a major aspect of our true nature.

When we **LEARN TO DISCERN** between what will support and empower us on our path and what will distract us, we notice when we are stuck and notice when we are in the flow, learning to distinguish between the two.

We can see the importance of **ACKNOWLEDGING OLD BELIEFS** as they are presented. If we notice we don't want to say something, it is a clue to start talking. It is important to own our speaking and **BE RESPONSIBLE** for the conversation. There is no one else out there. We can see everything as our reflection. Nothing would catch in our minds if we didn't already have a belief about it.

We learn to **SPEAK HONESTLY** from our hearts. When we speak honestly from our hearts it allows others to find their hearts too. It opens the space for miracles.

When we listen we can learn to **LISTEN** from a clear space with all that we are—our hearts, our bodies, our souls. When we listen to **HEAR THE HEART** in others we hear the truth they have to share.

We learn to see the brilliance in wanting what we have, not what we don't have. It is critical to develop our ability to **STAY PRESENT** in all aspects of the experiment. When we find that we are reflective about the past or daydreaming about some future—that something other than the present moment has captured our attention—that is an indication that we are not being present and our clue to come back to this moment. When we notice that we *want* something, which is distinctly different from being committed to something, as it implies an attachment to a thing—the object of our desire—this is another clue to bring us back to the present.

As we begin to **PRACTICE THE ART OF INCLUSION** we create our communities and support structure consciously. Everyone wants to come to the party. As we observe ourselves excluding anyone we are given insight into our intolerance and the opportunity to practice love.

First find the determination and willpower to keep going and then generate the discipline to find the determination and willpower to **KEEP GOING** day after day. Let our longing to discover our authenticity be our life's inspiration.

Let's **LIGHTEN UP!** We aren't that significant. After all there are six billion of us. As we perfect the art of **BEING HUMBLE** we open to that which is hidden from us in our self-importance.

HEART

> Listen quietly for signs of life inside the heart. Ah. . .yes! She's still there: you pounder of love; you mover of mountains; you and you alone have the power to still the mind! The body settles into One rhythm. . .that of Yours. . .steady. . .infinite. . . syncopation. . .Love opens Your doors into Oneness. . .I. . .who am . . .no body. . .no mind. . .all body. . .all mind. . .Lover. . . Beloved. . .pounder of rhythms.
>
> Madren Campbell

Heart consciousness is opening our hearts into remembrance. Love—love without conditions—lives in the heart. The grand experiment is a voyage into discovery that will show us just what it is that draws us forward into this journey. As we gain awareness and wisdom our hearts open naturally into a state of remembrance. This opening begins the return to Oneness—the remembering of who we have always been beneath our crystalline shells. Listen carefully to your heart. Its message is clear—open, open, open—Yes!

BE HONEST with others and with ourselves. What is it we really want? How much are we willing to risk? What do our hearts yearn for? What stops us from going after it? When we are willing to be totally honest we open the door to living from our hearts.

Allow ourselves to be **OPEN AND VULNERABLE**. It will be uncomfortable. If we choose to, we can do it despite the discomfort. Our openness and vulnerability unlocks the heart's door. The heart's door is only locked when we close down to protect ourselves. Open and the both the door and lock disappear.

When we see how we create our world we see that everyone is operating based on their own personal model of their world. Given that, none of us could do anything different than what we are doing—what is, is. What is there not to forgive? And, if we can think of something we might want to revisit our beliefs. People don't disappoint us. Our expectations disappoint us. Forgiveness creates a heart opening. True **FORGIVENESS** is the recognition that there is nothing to forgive.

COURAGE—it helps to have a little! Ha! The courage we are talking about is the courage to stand right in the middle of the vulnerability and openness no matter what the circumstance, to speak honestly from our hearts in those moments, and to keep being love, even though, depending on the circumstance, we may feel the need to protect, to defend, or if our pattern is one of leaving, to flee.

Give ourselves permission to **BE BOLD**—the freedom to experiment. It is a gift only we can give ourselves, and it is the gift that keeps on giving. Go ahead and push the limits; step outside of the comfort zone; get the adrenaline pumping; make big promises that will expand what is possible and challenge who we know ourselves to be. Remember, it is all a big experiment.

We learn the art of **COMPASSION** when we begin to realize that we all want the same thing. We all want to experience happiness for ourselves and others. We all want to experience the joy of living a full life. We all want to know satisfaction and the fulfillment of having loving relationships—of loving others and being loved by and cared for by others. We all want to give of ourselves and know that when we do it makes a contribution to someone or something worthwhile. This is how we **HONOR** ourselves and all others as ourselves. It is seeing the divine in all that is around us and knowing that we are that also.

We can find something to **BE GRATEFUL** for every day. It can be as simple as the sun going up and coming down. Express gratitude every day for the opportunities we have to experience and express love. As we practice finding something every day to be thankful for in our lives we create an ongoing awareness of gratitude.

These essentials are universally applicable within the context of the grand experiment. As we explore the myths and the alternative realities, these essentials will allow us to stay open and vulnerable to the possibilities created. As we learn to integrate them into our daily lives they will allow us to experience the new possibility at the level of our hearts rather than on a purely intellectual basis.

<u>5</u>
THE HOUSE OF CARDS

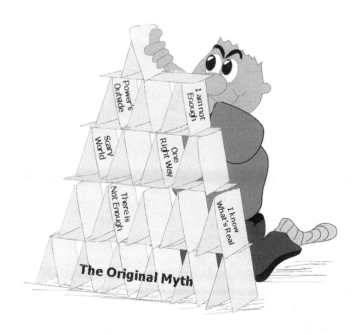

Underlying the six major myths is the seventh and original myth. These myths are reinforced by our accumulating beliefs and build on the foundation of our separation. They are the way we experience the original myth in our day-to-day lives. Living consistently and aligning our lives with these myths we fortify and validate our separate identity. These myths are mutually dependent, feeding on each other. Eliminate any one of the myths, and all the myths are suspect, including the original myth. Although other myths exist, these six are significant and affect us on a daily basis. They contribute to our inability to see beyond separation. These myths are the house of cards built upon the false foundation of the original myth. It is important to understand the complexity of these six myths and each one's alternative reality before we engage the original.

> Empty everything to come here, to this NOW. Empty everything you have ever done, empty every way you prefer and thus clutch. Unclutch your hold on this terra-formed heart of inspiration that is your ego. Now you are leveled to the ground of Good. Now the Great Rising can begin.
>
> Elle Collier Re

Our experiment will investigate each of the seven myths. When we are willing to see these myths as myths, we can wake up to the impact they have on each of us, and on our daily lives. Our willingness opens the door to see differently than we currently do. With this willingness we can see the myths from a perspective outside of the myths rather than being at the effect of them. This is a golden opportunity. In this opening of possibility we can then examine an alternative reality for each from this new perspective.

When we see our current life as a dynamic expression of the myths-in-action, we can use each experience to further understand how our beliefs determine our reality. By what we choose to believe, we make up the story of our life. As we continue to develop our awareness and understand that we can alter our beliefs, we have the ability to create a story in line with who we say we want to be.

> We must be able to see that the very root cause of suffering and pain is our insistence on maintaining ideologies centered on an individuality that doesn't exist. We are exactly like a ball of twine. If you unravel the twine to get to whatever is inside, you only end up with a pile of twine and empty space. When you unravel the ideas and beliefs that hold 'you' together, all that remains is empty space. There is no 'you' in the way that you think.[1]
>
> Aja Thomas

Each of these myths lives for us as either belief or as possibility. We will offer one possible reality for each myth. An infinite number exist—as many as there are human beings on the planet. We will merely open the door to a glimpse of what is possible. By extricating ourselves from our habitual myths, we are able to invent a future free from the limitation and encumbrances of fear, and the beliefs we previously empowered.

As we shift our beliefs a new possibility opens the potential for transformed behavior. Becoming aware and responsible for our beliefs allows us to peel away the myths that are in the background. As more and more layers are

---

[1] Aja Thomas, *In This Moment*, Teachings on the Nature of Consciousness, Atma Institute, 1999

exhumed what emerges is greater possibility for freedom of expression. Check out kids on the playground sometime. You'll see total animation, total freedom—total spontaneity. When we break free of the grip of our beliefs, this is the possibility for our own unlimited expression.

We can choose to be responsible, to own what is happening and what we are doing—with that comes complete freedom. This opens the possibility for the recognition that we truly do create our worlds and that life is indeed, a grand experiment.

MYTH #1—THE WORLD IS A SCARY PLACE

ROOT CHAKRA—SELF-PRESERVATION—*Pitfall: Fear*

> Got God on my side and I'm just trying to survive.
> But if what you do to survive kills the things you love,
> *Fear's a powerful thing.*
> It'll turn your heart black you can trust.
> It'll take your God-filled soul; fill it with devils and dust.
>
> Bruce Springsteen, <u>Devils and Dust</u>

The idea that the world is a scary place is born with the moment of separation, which is also the instant of movement from oneness to aloneness—approximately at age 2 to 4 depending on the opinion embraced. Researchers are finding that the moment may actually be much earlier. Through hypnotherapy and the rebirthing process research subjects have described going from at-one-ment with the mother to the experience of separation and shock as they emerge into a brightly lit room at the moment of birth. Whether it is at birth or at age 2 to 4, the movement is from oneness to aloneness.

The idea of a scary world is built and reinforced as we are taught how to protect ourselves from getting hurt and as we are trained in acceptable societal behavior. The motivation that drives the teaching and training is fear—fear that we will get hurt, fear that we won't fit in, fear that we won't succeed—basically fear that we won't be all right. This teaching is designed to instill fear in order to prevent harm.

This myth comes from the collective resonance, the cumulative vibrational frequency of all the people that have been on the planet since time began. The world truly was a scary place then, when a saber-tooth tiger might eat you if you made one mistake, or perhaps even if you did everything right. Now in this technical age our fear is more of a mental process than a physical reaction. The dog eat-dog world we now live in is the latest version of the prehistoric world.

Most of us aren't worried about our next meal, or a roof over our head, or being eaten by a tiger, but we live as though we will die, emotionally at least, if we aren't successful, if we don't look good, don't have the right stuff, or can't acquire our current desire. We worry that if we don't fit in, we will be excluded—a fate worse than death.

Fear has reinvented itself!

As we were writing this book I kept seeing this very large, very persistent fear. At first I hid it from Madren, Karen and myself, when I could manage it, but eventually it became too large. It turned into the elephant in the closet, trumpeting to get out.   What was the fear?   It had many levels but at the core it all came down to not wanting people to see the 'real me'.   If they knew they wouldn't listen to what I had to say.   If they saw my imperfection—the devils inside—they would know I had nothing to offer that they wanted.   Gayle G.

Yes, the world is a scary place. We see accidents on the freeway and know the odds are stacking up against us—we could be next. We watch television and see the story about the missing child, and we are afraid our children will be kidnapped, raped, and murdered. We even drive our kids to school or escort them to and from the bus. We carry our cell phones with us everywhere so that people can find us in case of emergency. We worry about cancer, heart disease, diabetes, MS, Alzheimer's, obesity—afraid we won't see old age—and we worry about wrinkles, aches and pains, a lingering death—afraid that we will. We worry about losing our home and our stuff—of being robbed, of having a fire, earthquake, flood and tornadoes—and buy loads of insurance for protection and then we worry that the insurance won't cover us if we need it. We worry about dirty bombs, biological weapons, suicide bombs, and the other toys of terror. We worry about losing our jobs, not having enough income to make the house payment, buy the food, pay the utilities, put gas in our tanks, or put some away for retirement. We've been counting on social security and our pensions and now we are worried they won't be there when we need them because we see them disappearing. We worry about not being comfortable and that we won't be able to maintain our preferred life-style.

Fear hooks us. It is an addictive habit. Our constant exposure to the messages of fear has numbed us to the point that what would have excited our nerves in the past no longer even dents our awareness.

Being numbed, we look for constantly increasing levels of stimulation so that we can feel more. At least, when we are reacting to fear we are feeling something, even if that something is anxiety. Perhaps that is why we stop to look at automobile accidents. The lanes always stop in both directions—one side stacked up behind the accident and the other side stopping to look. What are we looking for when we slow down and stare? What are we thinking? Next time this occurs you might notice for yourself.

Technology is our new safety net. Everyone has a cell phone. We are even giving them to our children. We are installing alarms on our homes, our cars and now we have alarms for the elderly, worn as a necklace or a wristband, so they are never far from help. Technological advances (email, cell phones, blackberries) are allowing us to be available and locatable 24/7. They are supposed to make us feel safer but in actuality, on an individual basis, we still feel more threatened than ever.

It is a vicious circle. Our fears make us skeptical. The skepticism leads to a lack of trust. Without trust we fear fully connecting with others. Our wireless may be connected but *we* do not appear to be connecting. The degree to which we hold back or withhold emotions, feelings, or communication because of the fear, is the degree to which fear has a grip on us and can therefore determine our behavior. We are enslaved and limited by the need to hide what is really going on with us because we aren't sure whom we can trust. The belief in a scary world is entwined around our physical, mental and emotional security—or lack there of. It creates the need to always be thinking about how to protect and defend ourselves.

A shift happens whenever my partner brings up having a baby. The shift is from my heart-centered awareness to my primal sense of survival. Can I provide for this family? Can I be responsible? My partner wants children and when she brings up the topic, I notice a distinct shift in the way I feel. I definitely tend to protect myself and defend my justification for postponing the decision. Madren C.

Here is what the little voice in our head might be saying: Look out! Caution! Be careful. Watch your back. Don't fully engage. Hold back a bit and don't show all your cards. Be careful or you'll get hurt. Don't trust anyone completely— keep a safe distance. Protect and defend!

LESSON—BOO!

<u>Purpose:</u> To bring awareness to how the myth—The World is a Scary Place—determines your decisions and behavior.

<u>Instructions:</u> Prepare to write your answers to the following questions:

1. What do I want to do or say that I don't because I am afraid?
2. What don't I want to do or say that I do because I am afraid?
3. How would it feel to share my feelings about this with others?
4. Has what I am afraid of shifted over the years? What causes my fear to change?

REALITY #1—THE WORLD 'IS'—WE GIVE IT MEANING

ROOT CHAKRA—SELF PRESERVATION—*Goals: Stability, Health, Trust*

> It is our mind that creates the world.
> The Buddha

Our interpretation creates our experience of this world. In this sense it is moldable and responsive to our beliefs. The universe is indifferent, but we can create, through our interpretation, a benevolent world even as bombs fall from the sky. People have lived in wretched situations—concentration camps, prisons, amid death and destruction—and allowed themselves to be in the presence of it. There is a powerful distinction that these people have made that we don't normally make. They released their expectation of the world being what they thought it should be and agreed to see it as it was. This allowed them to be true to themselves and their commitment to the quality of their own lives.

Victor Frankl survived the holocaust—one of the most horrific, fearful experiences that mankind has seen—by accepting responsibility for creating his own reality. The following quote provides a glimpse of his insight.

> We who lived in the concentration camps can remember the men who walked through the huts comforting others, giving away their last piece of bread. They may have been few in number, but they offer sufficient proof that everything can be taken from a man but one thing: The last of his freedoms—to

choose one's attitude in any given set of circumstances, to choose one's own way.[2]

Victor Frankl

It is our minds that invent the idea that we live in a scary world. We live in a world of life and death, joy and pain. Our judgments of good and bad create our experience. Yes, situations will arise that could cause us harm. When we are faced with a potentially harmful situation, the first step out of our automatic response to fear is to stop and recognize that we are operating from fear. Then we can see that what is required is discernment rather than reaction. It is at this point, we can determine a suitable course of action.

Cease! Halt! Alto! Discernment Required!!

Because we conceal our fears, even from ourselves, they operate subliminally, driving our decision process. Since we haven't allowed ourselves the luxury and taken the time necessary to get to know our fears intimately, we don't allow ourselves the gifts fear has for us. A thought, perhaps a

[2] Victor Frankl, Man's Search for Meaning, Washington Square Press, Simon and Schuster, New York, 1963.

House of Cards

warning pops into our head—don't do that—and we think, "Oh, that's right, I better not do that. Something bad could happen." And the thought stops us. We don't know what the outcome might have been. We empowered the thought from the fear and it stopped us from trying—it stopped us in our tracks. We never will know whether it could have been a great experience, a bad experience, or even a life-altering experience.

The fear doesn't stop us. It is our thought about the fear that stops us. Our thoughts, desires and fears do not have any power unless we empower them. Being able to discern the right action in the moment, an ability that we can all access when fear is not determining our behavior, empowers us to move purposely, powerfully—propelling us into life.

One facet of the fear that we feel is simply the resonance of past generations involved in fearful situations. Originally that fear arose when the beast was closing on us and our fight or flight response kicked in. Now that fear includes much that is truly not fearful. Yes, the resonance of fear is present. When fear appears, we merely need to see it, name it, make a decision based on the facts and act appropriately, and as we do we shift the resonance of the planet.

Fear does not exist when we are present in the moment. In the moment there is just the event unfolding. Our automatic reaction to the event (genetics, programming, and life experiences) determines our response. For most of us the automatic response is based in fear. That fear response provokes an interpretation of what has transpired and creates a story to support that interpretation. The whole process takes place in seconds, before we even have a chance to validate the stories being woven. As we pull more evidence from the past, whether it is true or not, it feels true. Something in us wants to believe it.

It is only if we take the moment to stop and analyze the facts that we can begin to untangle fantasy from reality, assumptions from fact. If we don't stop and question the story it stays a reality, at least in our minds, and then we act upon it not knowing whether we act from any true basis in fact or not. Our assumptions become hardened into fact very quickly.

John had been out of town for a week, came home late, and hadn't called during any of his layovers that day. My mind had started writing the story of John not caring. "Why didn't he call? Don't I matter? Is he pulling away again?" He came home during the night. Early in the morning I snuggled him and he didn't respond. "Why didn't he respond? Boy, he is really in his pull-away zone." Instantaneously I had an entire story written and it wasn't good. When we woke up John went downstairs and I decided to meditate because my head was in a real negative space. A voice said, "You've made all this up. Look at the whole story you have created." When I came out of meditation and found John in his office I shared all the crazy thoughts. He smiled and said, "I did call you. You were out." Downstairs the answering machine was blinking. Karen J.

When we go along for the ride with our thoughts, we create bigger and bigger whoppers. Usually the way the story plays out is that we either project the experience into the future, fearing a repeat and not wanting this to happen again, or we get stuck in the past reliving the experience—playing it in our heads over and over—like the movie *Groundhog Day*. The problem is created when we remain mired in our version of the story rather than moving through the pain and hurt. If we can allow ourselves to experience the pain or the hurt, we will not be tempted to create walls around ourselves for protection, walls that usually only succeed in walling us off from life instead of walling out the pain. In our need to protect ourselves from a painful experience, we can cut ourselves off from the love that can heal us.

As we play or wallow in our stories about fear, hell is lived here on earth. Hell isn't somewhere you go. It is right here, right now, and it's in bed with fear. Hell was created as a control mechanism designed to ensure conformity to a certain set of behaviors; our acceptance of the reality of hell programs us as fear receptacles. If hell exists, this is a scary world and there is much to fear. Once we see how we create this fear, we can also see that the often-quoted saying is right— "Pain is inevitable, suffering *is optional*." How we interpret our reality determines our level of suffering.

> Heaven has a road, but no one travels it;
> Hell has no gate but men will bore through to get there.
>   Chinese Proverb

Completely accepting everything that happens in our life, without blame and as our own creation, generates an opening into possibility. When we take ownership of our lives, we see the truth of our experience, as it is, and become conscious participants. No, it won't always be beautiful. It won't always be joyful and painless. It will still offer us the full spectrum of life. But, the suffering, the wanting it to be something else, anything else, will be gone. Said many ways: with acceptance comes the 'peace that passeth understanding' of Christianity, the 'right mindfulness' of Buddhism, 'the peace than comes with surrender' of Islam. When we stop resisting what is, heaven stares us in the face.

> Love is the total absence of fear. Love asks no questions. Its natural state is one of extension and expansion, not comparison and measurement. [3]
>
> Gerald G. Jampolsky, M.D.

When we stop our automatic response, our reaction to fear, what is left is the acceptance of what is, which is Love without conditions or said another way, our Wholeness. Our belief in a scary world keeps us from fully experiencing Wholeness. Is the world a scary place? No, not inherently. It is, only if we believe it is. We are the ones who choose.

---

[3] Gerald G. Jampolsky is an American psychiatrist, lecturer, and author. For more information visit his website at www.attitudinalhealing.org.

LESSON—CHOICE

Sit quietly and breathe in, breathe out. Concentrate on just breathing until you begin to relax. Breathe in. Breathe out. Breathe in. Breathe out. Focus your attention on the energy center at your root chakra, located near your tailbone. This chakra grounds you to this planet and your physical experience. It is the center of self-preservation. Picture the color red, which is the color associated with the vibrational frequency of the chakra, emanating out from your root chakra in energetic waves.

Red Light   Base

Sit with the energy until you can feel it. Within this chakra of self-preservation, see that you have the ability to discern appropriate choice. Trust your ability to make choices consistent with your authentic nature that will not only allow for your preservation but for the fulfillment of your life's purpose. Sit quietly and let the red energetic light and the word 'Choice' penetrate your awareness.

MYTH #2—THERE IS NOT ENOUGH

SACRAL CHAKRA—SELF-GRATIFICATION—*Pitfall: Guilt*

> **IN BABY BOOMLET, PRESCHOOL DERBY IS THE FIERCEST YET**
> NY TIMES, March 3, 2006
> The fierce competition for private preschool in New York City
> has been propelled to such a frenzy this year by the increased
> numbers of children vying for scarce slots that it could be
> mistaken for a kiddie version of "The Apprentice."

Fear is generated with the realization that as physical beings we need to survive. The imperative is '*I*' need to survive. We do not consider that, '*We*' need to survive. With the 'I' thought, the Whole is negated. There is no 'we'. The basic concern of each of us is to find enough for ourselves. If we consider other people, most likely it is to figure out how they can help us get what we want.

Prior to the agrarian era, humans hunted and gathered only what we could use at the time. We ate what was in season and followed the wild herds. We were nomads living off the land, gathering seasonally available foodstuff. With the advent of agriculture, we began raising our own foods, raising our own stock, and settled into areas best suited for this new activity, giving up the nomadic life-style for one more stationary. Soon to follow was our discovery that we could store many of the foods we needed to survive. Accumulating foodstuffs, the origin of wealth, was a natural next step. When we saw that others had more than we did, it created a new point of reference for us. Because they had more, we then wanted more. We justified our desire for more as need.

Perhaps we'd have a better chance to survive through a hard winter or a famine if we had more. We would have more control over our own destiny with more wealth (as accumulated food sources). That thought process grew like a snowball until it became what it is today.

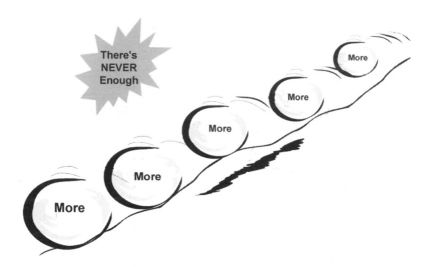

Our current observations tell us that scarcity is real. We can even find statistics to back it up. Everywhere populations are exploding. There is less available land; lower food and grain production; rising food, oil, housing and energy prices; less space for our car on the road.

STATISTICS[4]
➤ There is more human flesh on the planet than any other single species; as of 1999 we were at 6 billion as compared to 3 Billion in 1960. It took 800 years to grow from 500 million to 1 billion and only 130 years to grow from 1 billion to 2 billion
➤ World food and grain production peaks in the 1980's
➤ The US imports grain for the first time in 1988

---

[4] Thom Hartmann, The Last Hours of Ancient Sunlight, Three Rivers Press, 1999

> China imports food for the first time in 1995
> US topsoil down 30% since 1950, down 75% since the colonization of America
> 1500 acres of land become desert every hour largely due to the destruction of upwind forests
> 72 acres of rainforest are destroyed every minute; rainforests are the primary source of oxygen on the planet
> We lose 20% more of our crops to insects today than in 1945

Is there any reason why we should believe that there is enough? It doesn't look like there is. Perhaps there once was enough, but take a look at the numbers and it doesn't seem to add up to enough now.

In the United States, perhaps in an effort to convince others and ourselves that we have enough and don't have to worry, we are using more and more gas with bigger, more powerful vehicles. We are buying larger houses (some for part-time residential use), and we are consuming more per capita as a nation than any other place in the world. We judge enough by how much money we have, how much power we have, how many things we have, and whether or not they are the right things. But no matter how much we accumulate, it is not enough—regardless of our economic status.

Since September 11 the feeding frenzy has escalated. The response has been Buy—Buy—Buy! More—Better—Different! Build the nest egg. Our security was threatened and in response we have each in our own way created sanctuaries to protect us from harm. In the States many wealthy people are buying up properties outside of the U.S. for a safe haven far from the target of terrorists. Those of us for whom that isn't an option (almost all of us), have created sanctuaries in more simple ways, such as making certain we have more food on hand, reestablishing family relationships or by consciously or unconsciously sticking our heads in the sand. We are not secure enough—there is not enough safety here to stake our future on. Safety is scarce.

We live as if there is no scarcity, but the talk in our heads, and what drives our behavior, is scarcity. We are constantly watching out for ourselves, making sure we get our share, and taking care of number one. We know that there's not enough, so we better make sure we get our share first or we might lose out. We better make sure that there's enough for our future too! We don't want to lose what we have. We don't want to be without. If we lose it, we may not be able to replace it. We might end up penniless, living under the city bridge with the homeless.

When we look at our checkbooks we gulp—the balance is going down while prices are going up. Credit card offers arrive with the mail on a regular basis. Most of us have several cards and many are maxed out. There is always something new we must have. Just as soon as we take care of one desire, another replaces it. When we buy something new we say, "This sure is getting expensive. The last time I bought this I only paid half this much."

We pay for a military complex to keep us safe and have enought nuclear weapons to blow up the world several times over—and still don't feel safe enough. We are willing to stay in unhealthy relationships and work situations longer than we should, fearing that we'll lose what we have and that we won't be able to replace it with something as good. We are bombarded with ad campaigns using scarcity as one of their chief motivational tools—hurry sale ends tomorrow—only 30 left—prices are going up—this price won't last!

We were on a trip of a lifetime, headed south to Mexico on our sailboat. We had decided to follow our dream while we were still healthy. Off the coast of Oregon I said to Ken, "Man, I have to get a job." The thought passed—at least it passed into the background rather than staying in the foreground. Later, in Monterey, Ken came back to the boat and said, "Man, I have to get a job. I can't keep seeing it all go out and nothing coming in." We had money in the bank and were afraid of losing it—watching it slip away. The fear thoughts came and went throughout the year that we were gone and those thoughts were a large part of why we returned home when we did. We justified it other ways, but it was all about scarcity. We came back from Mexico planning to go north to Alaska for the summer. When we got back to Portland, Ken started working again. We didn't go. We didn't call it fear, but it was. We had money left and we could have gone if we wanted to, but we had less money left than what we felt comfortable having. We had reached the bottom of our tolerance level for our savings account. We didn't call that fear either, but it was. It was fear of not having enough money. Gayle G.

If we all look at what we are afraid of right now, what scarcity is all about, it comes down to the mother of all fears—the fear of dying. That never shows up in a conversation, but look at it. Why are we afraid to be penniless? Why are we afraid to lose our creature comforts? Why are we afraid to not have a roof over our heads? Why are we afraid to not have a full refrigerator? We are afraid that we won't be able to survive or that it will be so miserable, so uncomfortable that we won't want to live anymore.

Here is what the little voice in our head might be saying: I better make sure I have enough for my family and myself. There are never enough hours in the day. I don't have enough energy to do that; I'd better be smart this time. We don't have enough money for that; it costs too much. It was hard enough getting here in the first place. I sure don't want to start over again; there isn't enough time. I would give more if I had more to give. I should get a (better) job. I need to make more money. I can't retire now; I am going to have to work another ten years.

LESSON—MORE IS BETTER!

<u>Purpose:</u> To develop an awareness of how the myth—There is Not Enough—impacts your choices and the roles it plays in your life.

<u>Instructions:</u> Prepare to write down your answers to the following questions:

1. What do I think I must have to live?
2. What causes me to be less generous than I would like to be?
3. How much do I think is *enough*? What causes *enough* to change?

REALITY #2–THERE IS ABUNDANT POTENTIAL

THE SACRAL CHAKRA–SELF-GRATIFICATION—*Goals: Feeling, Pleasure, Healthy Sexuality*

The belief that there are not enough resources for everyone is one point of view. It has nothing to do with reality. We can live our lives as if there is not enough or we can live our lives as if there is abundance. Our actions will be consistent with our choices. If we choose to believe that there is not enough we will act in ways that separate us from each other, in ways that prevent others and ourselves from having what we want. If we choose abundance we have the ability to act in ways that bring people together and create Oneness. When we come from abundance we can include everyone. We can work together for cooperative solutions. Exclusion is an integral part of not enough. Within the exclusion mindset, we work in isolation from others focused on similar objectives, trying to reap the sole benefit for our group or ourselves. One choice creates further abundance, tapping into the potential the universe offers. The other stops the flow of abundance and limits what is available. Thinking about not enough as reality, creates the condition called not enough. The idea of not enough is a function of fear and plays into and validates our belief in the original myth.

I was out of town on business during the flood of 1996. We lived in a condo on the river at the time. Ken and I were in constant conversation about the rising water. He had rigged up a measuring device so that he could tell how far the

*water was from the deck and entry into our living room. He
knew how fast the river was rising and also knew when it was
slowing down. Ken invited friends over and had a pizza party.
They were there ready to act if necessary but were actually
having a fun boy's night in. When he talked about it later it
sounded like he had the time of his life. The news even came
by and interviewed him. He didn't expect they would be back.
He didn't give them the anxiety and fear they were looking
for. They would have preferred to interview our neighbors
but they weren't home. The neighbors on either side of us
had rented trucks and moved their furniture to safety. One
even removed the cabinets and moved them to the upper story
just to be safe. Ken never felt unsafe. He believed that
everything would work out all right but had a backup plan in
place just in case. For the neighbors there was no safe place
on the island. They had access to the same facts but in
the middle of the fear, couldn't see more creative solutions.
Gayle G.*

As long as we think there is not enough, there never will
be. We will behave consistent with the existence of scarcity
and make decisions based on that reality. We will not think
beyond the parameters that we have set. Our thoughts create
our reality. If we view the world as abundant, it is; if we
view the world as scarce, it is scarce, but it still holds its
potential for abundance. It is only our incomplete
understanding and point of view that sets limits. There is a
finite amount of water on the planet, but is there enough water
for everyone? The point is not whether there is enough water
on the planet or not. The point is *who* we choose to be and

where we are coming from in regards to the relationship between others, ourselves and the resources available to us. The question that begs an answer is, "Are we going to share or are we going to horde?" How we answer sets reality in motion.

When we share our marbles, we all get to play the game!

Thinking we know what resources are available cuts us off from access to possibilities beyond our current understanding. If we consider the possibility that we may have a limited viewpoint or belief of what is possible regarding abundance, unaware that we are missing important pieces of the picture, we open doors to solutions previously unknown. By tapping into the potential that exists, we can provide ourselves and others with more than we could ever need.

In the mid-nineties I was audited by the IRS for two previous years and they decided that I owed back taxes. My accountant said that they were mistaken and that I didn't owe any money.

We re-filed returns for the years in question and the local IRS officer declined to accept the submissions. The result was a declaration against me of $40,000 in back taxes. Out of my conversations with my accountant and the notes that the local IRS agent sent us, my experience was that all I could do was pay. I knew that the information wasn't accurate and it didn't seem fair, but I didn't know how to correct it and so I didn't do anything. I avoided taking care of it for several years. At the end of that timeframe I consulted another accountant who said the only option available was to offer compromise. Since he was my expert I proceeded to fill out the necessary forms and follow his advice, some of which didn't ring true for me. The whole time I was scared to contact the IRS directly. I believed what the accountants and others had told me. I believed that the IRS didn't care about me; they just wanted the money and would be inflexible and take whatever I had. My behavior during this time became consistent with what I was told about the IRS, fearing that they would take whatever I managed to acquire, financially or materially. So I stopped participating in the world. I didn't own a house. I had an older, inexpensive automobile. I disconnected myself completely from the grid. The IRS became the bad guy, a source of fear. After three years and no acceptable result with my new accountant, the compromise came back rejected. I had reached my wits end. My experts had failed me. The next morning I woke up and realized that I had been avoiding my responsibility for handling this myself and had been blaming the accountants for not getting this done. I had deferred my responsibility to them. I realized the high cost of living under that umbrella for so many years and *the suffering was enough. I needed to be responsible and no matter what happened, I would be the one to talk with the IRS and get this thing completed. With this new awareness I dialed the IRS's 800 number. During my phone conversation I discovered that the tax advocacy branch could help me with my situation. The agent recommended that I call them and gave me the number. The long and short of it was that within two months the whole thing was complete and even included a small refund. My shift to 'being' responsible opened the door to solutions previously unseen by me. Madren C.*

We just have to change our thinking to include the idea of abundance. There are already enough alternate fuel sources, when further deployed, to replace reliance on fossil fuels. There is and has been enough food to feed each one of us on the planet.

ISN'T HUNGER JUST A QUESTION OF DISTRIBUTION?

No. Almost every location on earth can produce enough food for its population. Even Bangladesh is self-sufficient in food production. The challenge is that people cannot earn enough to buy the food that is available.

The Hunger Project[5]

What else is possible is yet to be seen. Seeing the possibility in this new paradigm will require that we see through the fear that drives our scarcity mentality.

---

[5] The Hunger Project is a global strategic organization committed to the end of world hunger. For more information visit their website at www.thp.org.

WHOLENESS IN THE WORLD

1. Make up three sack lunches. Put them in your automobile or backpack and hand them out to strangers in need.

2. Find the closest homeless shelter and prepare and serve dinner.

3. Go work at your local food bank. Ask questions to understand the need in the community; ask them "How can I be of service?"

4. Volunteer at the humane society and hug a bunch of puppies. Take as many for a walk as you can.

5. Donate your time at a nursing home reading stories and listening to the people who would love a little attention and caring.

6. Be a Big Brother or Big Sister. Show children the possibility.

7. Listen to someone you disagree with and give them a hug.

8. Pick up trash whenever you see it.

9. Work on yourself; love others. Don't mix up the two. See the beliefs that stand in your way of seeing the divine within all.

LESSON—WHOLENESS

Sit quietly and breathe in, breathe out. Concentrate on just breathing until you begin to relax. Breathe in. Breathe out. Breathe in. Breathe out. Focus your attention on the energy center at your sacral chakra, located between your pubic bone and your belly button. This chakra grounds you emotionally to this planet and your physical experience. It is the center of self-gratification. Picture the color orange, which is the color associated with the vibrational frequency of the chakra, emanating out from your sacral in energetic waves.

Orange Light　　　　　　　　　　　　　　　　　　**Sacral**

Sit with the energy until you can feel it. Within this chakra of self-gratification, unlimit your thinking to include concern for the Whole, and know the potential for abundance is real. Sit quietly and let the orange energetic light and the word 'Wholeness' penetrate your awareness.

MYTH #3—THE POWER IS OUTSIDE OF US

SOLAR PLEXUS CHAKRA—SELF-DEFINITION—*Pitfall: Shame (Shows up often as Blame)*

Primal man experienced lightening and thunder, earthquakes and volcanoes, catastrophic events, predators both human and beast. It was just the way it was. His neocortex was not developed sufficiently to allow further analysis. As his ability to think and reason developed, man innocently invented gods to explain what he couldn't explain in the world around him and to justify the chaos and the randomness of what he saw. The gods were the answer to those things out of man's control.

With his creation of the gods, mankind set the stage to hand over control of his life to something outside of himself. The power wasn't within us—it was outside of us. It rested with the medicine man, the shaman—the person who could talk directly to the gods. In a world filled with power struggles this once innocent idea—the invention of gods—turned into a method and means of control with one goal, control of the masses and the resources available to them.

We have given our power away or had it taken from us. We have given it to those we deemed as most powerful—the clan leader, the kings and queens, the lord of the manor, the company owner or boss, our husbands, our wives, our children, our teachers, our parents, our political leaders, our religious advisers—and by our permission we gave them authority over our lives. Sometimes we were willing. Sometimes we were not. It may not have appeared as permission, yet it was. Fear is a powerful incentive.

How did this mostly unquestioned practice begin? If we were banished from the clan we were pretty much guaranteed a quick death. Banishment was one of the first control mechanisms put into place socially. It controlled behavior and gave power to the few who had the brute strength or the advantage of numbers to enforce the decree. In order to survive, we agreed that we needed protection and that there was safety in acquiescing to the will of the leader.

The fear energy that kept clan members in line still exists. Over the years it has grown and now includes all the fear energy that has ever existed. Energetically, it grows in strength moment by moment. We are 'judging machines', constantly discerning what is safe and what is not in our environment and our experience. Every time we judge ourselves or judge others, we perpetuate the fear energy on the planet.

Our childhoods, regardless of how well meaning our

parents, reinforced this myth. The power was with the parent. Grounding, physical discipline, extra chores, and withholding of allowance were all means of keeping the power in the hands of the parent. The power was with the teacher. Staying after school, additional homework, a visit to the principle, sitting out in the hall, or having to write, "I will not _____" on the blackboard a hundred times, were all means of maintaining control.

We learned at a young age who really had the power. The power was with anybody except us. We were too young or too old, too dumb or too smart, too big or too small, but never just right—never perfect just the way we were. If we tried to express our power it brought sad, uncomfortable, sometimes hurtful, consequences.

When I was a little kid, two friends and I witnessed a fight between two of the older boys. We were in the 3rd grade. The older kids were much older—they were 6th graders. One of the older boys, Rocky, was the school bully. He was big and a little bit fat. The kid he was fighting, Johnny, was shorter and skinny. Johnny didn't stand much of a chance. As the three of us watched together in horror it got really bad and we began trying to figure out what we could do. One of us suggested getting a branch and hitting Rocky with it so Johnny could get away. Almost instantaneously another of us said, "No, we can't do that. He might grab us and beat us up too." So we stood and watched from the sidelines feeling incapable of doing anything to stop it. I even said to Rocky, "Come on. He is already down; he's not getting up. It's over." And he said to me, "It's not over 'til I say it's over." My friend Michael

asked Rocky, "What's he going to do from down there?"
That's when he shocked us by peeing all over the kid. As he
did, he said, "Not much now." This really scared us and we
ran away, leaving Johnny lying on the ground crying, with
Rocky standing over him. We couldn't stop it and we felt
helpless and unable to help Johnny. We were even too scared
to try. In fact, he had told us not to tell anyone or we would
get the same, so for the rest of the week we stayed away from
any place we might run in to Rocky.   He had the power.
Madren C.

With this training we learned how to give our audience
what they wanted—regardless of whether or not it rang true
within us. Some of us learned to please, learning to do
whatever was necessary to survive—to get by. Those of us
who were 'successfully' socialized learned valuable lessons,
some which still work for us today, like consideration for
others or telling the truth. We also learned some other lessons,
like manipulation and dishonesty, which stand in the way of
our authenticity and set the framework, at least in our own
minds, of our unworthiness.

Those of us that didn't learn to please created another
framework within which to operate. That framework came
with an entire set of behaviors and consequences of its own.
The rebels, the loners, the nonconformists, are examples of
alternative frameworks. Whether we were a pleaser or a rebel,
the point is that we were reacting to something we had given
power to outside of ourselves—our parents, our teachers, or
society as a whole.

Some religious sects cemented this myth by positioning

the church as an intermediary between the individual and God. They became the direct link, requiring us to use them as the way to reach God. It was a natural outcome. We were powerless and needed someone to help us find the way. The power was outside of us, and the fire and brimstone was a great deterrent. The few who took and continue to take a dissenting stand pay a high price.

Whether we personally agree with these religious interpretations or not, we feel the repercussions of the beliefs through society's determination of moral values. Many of our laws are created as a result of these same moral judgments and passed down to us. Today's battles over sexual preference, abortion, and right-to-die are all cases in point.

This myth doesn't even surface as an issue for most of us until we experience a problem and the solution appears to be in someone else's hands. Usually the problem involves not getting what we want. As a result, we decide that since we can't make an impact or solve the problem, we are powerless. Within this powerlessness we shift our frustration and upset outward, blaming something, someone outside of ourselves. Listen to your thoughts next time you are stuck in traffic, waiting in line, can't access good health care, get your tax bill, or are standing at the gas pumps. We don't usually think about the power being outside of us until we want control over something and feel that we don't have it and can't get it.

The consequence of making that decision is that we separate ourselves from the source of our ability to solve the problems ourselves, and to have life be the way we want it or think we want it to be. This then keeps reinforcing the notion that something or someone else is that source and we are not.

With that decision, the power to solve the problem is indeed outside of us.

Here is what the little voice in our head might be saying: You said you'd do that, but you didn't. You've let me down. Once again, I can't count on you; I can't count on anyone. Why do they always make me do this? What's the point of saying anything; nothing will change. I should be able to count on you. I should have more say in what happens in my family, my community, my government, my life... Everything is just so messed up. The system sucks. There's no way to win. It's hopeless. What did I do God? Why are you punishing me?

LESSON–CONTROL GAME

<u>Purpose:</u> To bring awareness to those areas in your life where you are at the effect of the myth—The Power is Outside of Us.

<u>Instructions:</u> Prepare to write down your answers to the following questions:

1. Where do I feel that I lack some degree of power in my life?

2. What is it that causes me sometimes to feel that I am at the mercy of life's circumstances?

3. How is it possible to be in control sometimes and not others?

REALITY #3—THE POWER IS WITHIN

THE SOLAR PLEXUS CHAKRA—SELF-DEFINITION—
Goals: Vitality, Spontaneity, Purpose, Self-Esteem, Strength of Will

> If God is not in us, he never existed.
>
> Voltaire

Yes, mankind did invent god, but we invented god in 'our image'. We invented the gods in our awe of the unexplainable. We are made in the image and likeness of God, but not the god we invented. This may sound incredible to you but consider the possibility that we are the Universal Life Force, the Source of All, the Field, the Ground of All Being— Oneness.

Each of us is born capable and able. We each have a knowingness that we have not begun to tap into or understand. At some deep level we know that the answers are within us, that we are responsible for our own reality, that we are not victims of life but create it. An outside source, outside ourselves, does not and cannot decide our worth.

We do indeed have access to the wisdom we need in any given moment. It is available to us whenever we choose to listen. The power is within us to interpret every event in our lives. We already do this, all the time. We are hardwired to interpret each event as it happens. We react for a purpose— tied to keeping us safe in this world. It is our instinctual reaction to survive. We react to the threat—physical, mental, emotional, real or perceived—to our well-being. We make it mean something. The point is not whether or not we react but how we react—because we are going to react—but we have complete choice of what meaning we assign situations and we each have any number of meanings that we can attribute to them. We are the only one that makes it mean anything, not the other guy—just us. The choice we have is in the meaning we choose. Will we choose a meaning that elicits our automatic response, the one we typically have chosen in the past, or will we choose a meaning that elicits actions more consistent with how we say we would like to live our lives?

THE POSSIBLE DREAM

Often lost amid the cacophony of the 20th century's cannon roar and bomb explosions are the stories of people and movements that used nonviolent resistance against all odds to defeat ferocious opponents—to oust a tyrant in Chile, to thwart the Nazi's designs on Denmark, or to transform a South African political system that had denied rights to people of color. Entire societies from the Philippines to Poland have been radically transformed, suddenly or gradually, by those who refused to submit to arbitrary rule...Their ultimate goals were to overturn brutal regimes (South Africa), obstruct invaders (Denmark), or compel rights to be honored (Nashville)...Irrevocably altered were basic ideas about the nature of power.[6]

Peter Ackerman

Throughout history individuals have listened to their hearts' wisdom and taken action for a cause when they saw the need. They saw injustice that they could not let stand. In 1930, Mahatma Gandhi found the unifying principle of a salt march that began the movement for an independent India; In

---

[6] Peter Ackerman, A Force More Powerful, WETA. For more information visit the website www.forcemorepowerful.com.

1960, inspired by Gandhi's nonviolent legacy, James Lawson, a young Ohio minister, organized the Nashville sit-ins that began the desegregation of the lunch counters and fueled the equal rights movement in the United States; Lech Walesa, a shipyard electrician, in 1980, led a group of Polish workers in a stand for worker's rights that led to nationwide strikes and a solidarity movement that eventually resulted in the fall of Communism in that country. These individuals saw injustice and took power into their own hands, refusing to let fear and beliefs stop them from taking committed action.

Katrina struck the Gulf Coast and I was glued to the television. My heart was breaking for the people caught in the hurricane. I would sit and watch the news, hoping that we had somehow gotten a handle on the rescue effort and that those in need had gotten medical attention, food and water. I found myself using 'should' a lot. They should have gotten help there sooner; they should have known they would need to help the poor and sick evacuate; big oil should share in the sacrifice and be generous in support of their communities; they should... Friday morning, five days after Katrina made landfall, I told my husband, I can't keep using 'should'. I have to find what I can do myself. When I moved beyond 'should' I found the words to write a reply to the NY Times Op-Ed column with my thoughts. I made a donation to the Red Cross, and I prayed for our nation and all of its people, including those tasked with the imposing rescue effort. I released my reliance on others and listened to my inner knowing for direction. Gayle G.

When we listen carefully, we are
already tuned in perfectly.

The radios of the past allowed the pure unfiltered message to come through; they didn't filter out interference and static. At a subconscious level, we are actually more like those old radios. We tune to our favorite channel, the channel that has always determined our beliefs, thoughts, reactions and choices, yet there are other channels always playing in the background—with other meanings and other choices. We are capable of receiving multiple frequencies at any one time. Sometimes these frequencies do overlap and we receive multiple messages, even if we can't consciously make out the true nature of the message. Intuition is an example of this. When this happens we normally listen to the message we are most comfortable with, while we dismiss the overlapping or secondary message that may tend to be unfamiliar to us. If we stop and listen, we are able to consciously comprehend the quieter message in the background. This is the channel that the great teachers have always been able to access—the channel of Oneness. It is what allows us to know, at a deep level, that there is something more, and that we are all intimately connected.

I was in San Diego to sell my boat. I was tired and thoughts were flying in and out of my head and I noticed a tendency towards the negative. The thoughts were filled with anxiety and fear of not having it turn out the way I wanted. I also noticed how I was feeling. I felt heavy and de-energized. I heard the thought, "Man, you are so uptight and tense. Where did the enthusiasm go," so I grabbed my journal and began to write, "When I am not passionately going for it, when I am being a victim, I can count on my thoughts to be negative— poor me—blaming others—the power is outside of me." I had forgotten for the moment that I am completely responsible for my life, for my thoughts that I empower. When I turn back to being love, letting go of resisting things, letting go of needing things to be a certain way, opening my heart to understanding, compassion, love and not knowing, my joy and enthusiasm returns and love starts flowing through me as well. Madren C.

If we are willing to consider this possibility we begin to understand that we create our world moment-by-moment, with each and every choice of interpretation we make. The power is within and it always has been.

LESSON—LISTEN

Sit quietly and breathe in, breathe out. Concentrate on just breathing until you begin to relax. Breathe in. Breathe out. Breathe in. Breathe out. Focus your attention on the energy center at your solar plexus chakra, located a couple of inches above the navel. This chakra grounds you to your personal power on this planet. It is the center of self-definition. Picture the color yellow, which is the color associated with the vibrational frequency of the chakra, emanating out from your solar plexus in energetic waves. Sit with the energy until you can feel it.

Yellow Light   Solar Plexus

Within this chakra of self-definition, know that the answers are within. Our wisdom is always present and available. We merely have to listen. Sit quietly and let the yellow energetic light and the word 'Listen' penetrate your awareness.

MYTH #4—WE ARE NOT ENOUGH

HEART CHAKRA—SELF-ACCEPTANCE—*Pitfall: Grief* *(Shows up often as Self-Judgment)*

The idea that we are not enough is passed from generation to generation. With the original experience of not being sufficient to every circumstance and task, judgment occurred and laid the foundation for constant and continuous correction. This led to each individual's eventual understanding that not only were their actions not enough, they too must not be enough.

The doctrine of a wrathful God perpetuated and amplified the myth that we were not only insufficient but inadequate, and that our natural instincts were not okay. We would not have fallen prey to the doctrine if we hadn't already had an experience of being insufficient and from that experience decided that there was something missing. We sensed the thing that was missing, if supplied, would allow us to be sufficient and began our search to find the missing link in an infinite number of ways. That which was missing created an emptiness in us and we attempted to fill the void.

Religion provided an answer—if you were adequate God would be pleased with you; you need to make yourself more pure, more adequate to God. The doctrine, at varying levels, rang true for societies influenced by organized religion, regardless of whether or not individuals within that society chose to conduct their search within the framework of religion.

As humans evolved, so did their morals, standards and rules. These rules established the conflict between what was socially acceptable and what wasn't. The individual had a choice to conform to what was acceptable and be included, which felt closer to adequate, or to risk exclusion. What was acceptable natural behavior became restricted by the redefined social standards. Over time by agreement, new social standards became a norm for behavior in each society and generated a new reference point for self-judgment, from which we determined whether or not we were enough. The new standards didn't change our basic nature and in many ways conflicted with it, so our conflicting behaviors didn't stop— they just went underground.

If you add in the possible validity of morphogenetic theory which Quantum science supports today, then all the experiences from past generations, in the form of information, influence and affect us. Briefly the theory of morphogenetic fields goes as follows: Morphogenetic fields are basically nonphysical blueprints that give birth to forms. A morphogenetic field carries only information, not energy, and is available throughout time and space without any loss of intensity after it has been created. Morphogenetic fields are created by the patterns of physical forms (including such things as crystals as well as biological systems). They help guide the formation of later similar systems where a newly forming system tunes into a previous system by having within it a seed that resonates with a similar seed in the earlier form.

Morphic resonance, in Sheldrake's view, is 'the influence of like upon like through space and time.' He believes these fields (and he thinks there are many of them) are different than electromagnetic fields because they reverberate across generations with an inherent memory of the correct shape and form. The more we learn, the easier it is for others to follow in our footsteps.[7]

Lynne McTaggart

Many scientists are now exploring what has become known as the 'field', and discovering the possibility that the field is a receptive channel for all energetic vibration and information.

Harold S. Burr (Yale University) who studied and measured electrical fields around living things, specifically salamanders, discovered that salamanders possessed an energy field shaped like an adult salamander, and that this blueprint even existed in an unfertilized egg. Burr also discovered electrical fields around all sorts of organisms, from molds, to salamanders and frogs, to humans. Changes in the electrical charges appeared to correlate with growth, sleep, regeneration, light, water, storms, the development of cancer—even the waxing and waning of the moon. [7]

Lynne McTaggart

These vibrations consist of all frequencies, including the frequency of fear which stores our anxiety about our own worth, and explains why we have fear about things we have never personally experienced. We are constantly tuned into the fields and adapting our behavior to the information found within them. As Sheldrake said, this information helps guide the formation of later similar systems. Our ancestors who experienced being not enough and not okay in the past inform our current development and increase the odds of our feeling inadequate today.

---

[7]Lynne McTaggart, The Field, HarperCollins Publishers, 2002

As toddlers, when the attention was noticeably shifted off of us for the first time we had that initial experience of being not enough and it was not okay. This started a pattern of behavior involving one attempt after another to regain the attention. Something was missing. Instead of behaving in ways that were authentic to us, we started behaving in ways that compromised our authentic nature in order to please others and to experience being enough again. This pattern generally lasts a lifetime. It will take varying shapes and guises but will stem from this one moment in time.

As small children we were taught the difference between bad and good. Most of what we heard was training as correction. On a basic day-to-day level it didn't feel good when we were corrected instead of praised by those we wanted to please. We oriented our behavior around doing those things that would gain us praise and acknowledgment and away from those behaviors that received correction. The training was strong and was reinforced by the fact that praise felt good, reminding us of the time when we were enough, and correction didn't feel good, reinforcing the decision we had made that we were not enough.

When I was a 4ᵗʰ grader I had this idea that I needed to prove to everyone that I was smart. I went through all the books in my parent's book cupboard and selected several that would do the trick. I carried them to school and took them with me everywhere I went for that next week. Obviously (to me now) I was afraid that I wasn't smart enough or at least afraid that others wouldn't see how smart I was. Regardless of the reason, I had grabbed onto the idea that I had something to prove. As I walked around with the books I knew I was a fraud. I didn't call it that, but I knew that it didn't feel good and it only made it worse that nothing changed. The only thing I got out of the deal was a sore back and the knowledge that I wasn't smart enough to convince others how smart I was. I didn't get the attention I wanted and afterwards, I was even more certain that I was not enough. Gayle G.

Some of those things we were disciplined for seemed to come naturally. We were genuinely curious and wanted to experience the world around us. We found that playing doctor with the neighbor kids was bad; our parents' reaction made that very clear. We became confused—the messages didn't quite make sense. What satisfied our natural curiosity and what we were being taught were out of sync. We couldn't figure out why exploring our world—what we naturally wanted to do—was considered bad, unless we were bad. We knew that not only were we not enough; we would never be enough. Once we decide we are not enough, our life becomes about trying to be enough despite knowing we never will.

We look out into the world at what is presented as the ideal standard, and compare ourselves to what we've determined this to be, and invariably fall short. Addictive behaviors are prevalent in an attempt to either be enough or in reaction to the hopelessness of not being enough.

We amass material possession and financial wealth as a substitute for what is lacking inside or go the opposite direction, and spurn anything having to do with the status quo. We fight for attention, needing it from the outside; self-love is elusive. Others may tell us that we are wonderful or that we are the best, but we are unable to see past our self-doubt and self-judgment. We see others as whole and worthy, but not ourselves.

We look for our better half, our other half (the very fact that we consider ourselves a half is evidence of not being enough). There is a picture in our heads of how life should be: what we should look like, how smart we should be, what we should have. We constantly compare ourselves to others we deem to have made it or to our story of what it looks like to have made it. This standard is a moving target. As we approach it, it moves further away. We update and reinvent the criteria, raising the bar continually. We designed our acceptable standards, unwittingly, to reinforce the myth.

Here is what the little voice in our head might be saying: Just being 'me' is not enough. If being who I am isn't enough, I need to do something to prove my worth. No matter how hard I try, I just can't win. Nothing works. I don't care anymore. If I don't care, why does this feel so bad?

LESSON—TO BE OR NOT TO BE

<u>Purpose:</u> To bring awareness to how the myth—We are Not Enough—determines your decisions and behavior.

<u>Instructions:</u> Think back to events or circumstances that made you feel less than someone else, or that made you feel as if you were not enough. Go back as far as you can in your life. You may want to start with the most recent experiences and work backwards.

1. Pick two events and describe in writing with as much detail as possible, what happened.

<u>Instructions:</u> Write the answers to the following questions for each of the above events:

1. What were the decisions I made about myself?
2. What were the decisions I made about other people?
3. What did I decide about the world around me and how I fit into it?
4. How did I alter my behavior as a result of what I decided?

REALITY #4—WE ARE COMPLETE AND ENOUGH

THE HEART CHAKRA—SELF-ACCEPTANCE—*Goals: Balance, Compassion, Fulfilling Relationships*

Who we are is appropriate to our level of development as we continue to evolve in each and every moment. Our evolution is not optional. It is occurring continuously whether we choose it or not. Self-judgment is measuring ourselves against both an internal and external standard, regardless of whether we have ever met the standards. Depending on our perception we decide how we fit on the scale of capable and able, complete and enough.

The mind's job is to judge, to separate and label, to classify and quantify. The mind will always do its job and it does its job so well that we are convinced that we are limited to its workings—that we too, can be classified and labeled. We each classify and label based on our individual reference points thus far in life; so everyone's reference point is different. Since we are constantly adding to our life experiences, that reference point is a living, breathing target. Enough is not a fixed thing. It grows, expands and contracts as we do. Despite our belief in the programming we are exposed to, the dynamic of enough and our development are shifting and changing constantly. As we classify and label, we attempt to limit the limitless, not realizing that we cannot be limited.

There is a distinction between doing enough to get enough and just being enough. If we are coming from the domain of doing we have to get the right stuff and do the right things to find happiness and fullness as we attempt to increase the quality of our lives. The mind thinks that if it has the things that we see in the media then our lives will be like the dreams that the advertisers wrap around the things they want us to buy. As long as we come from the domain of doing, we are never enough. Enough, like us, will always evolve. It will grow to include whatever is desired in the moment.

There is another domain in which life occurs—the domain of being. It is 'Who' we are naturally. It comes with distinguishing that we are more than a doing machine, that the Whole is more than the sum of its parts. This is the recognition that we are spiritual beings not human doings. Being creates the context in which all the doing occurs. It comes with the package of being human. We are not trained to be; we are trained to do. When we attempt to be, we generally attempt to do being, rather than realize that there is nothing we have to 'do' in order to 'be'. Being is what we are and as we accept this and acknowledge that we are Whole and complete, we are living in the domain of being regardless of what we do, and being Whole and complete is always enough.

For years I had wanted my son to change his life and be different. I couldn't admit this to myself openly, but I knew it was what I wanted. I didn't realize it at the time but it wasn't about him; it was about me. I had decided that I was a bad mother because he didn't live a conventional life. I didn't tell him what I was thinking. He might have walked out of my life as my older son had done for four years. The thought of going through that again was terrifying. I was supportive and loving on the surface but it didn't feel good when I saw him do or say things that I didn't agree with. I felt I had failed as a mother. When I realized that I had an agenda for his life and he wasn't fitting into it, I consciously chose to let go of my expectations and just love him the way he was, to give him the freedom I would want in his position, and in fact, wanted from my own family. When I finally let that go and just loved him unconditionally, knowing that he was complete and whole just the way he is, our relationship shifted exponentially. The need for him to be any way other than the way he was vanished and possibilities that were closed to us opened. I could love my son freely, freed from my paradoxical desire to see myself as a perfect mother all the while knowing I wasn't. I was complete and enough too. The guilt dissolved. And, in my pure, unconditional love for him, I freed him to do the same. In that instant, there was freedom to be anything we wished. Gayle G.

In reality we are beings who are capable and able, complete and enough just as we are, independent of anything and everything that we buy or do, have or don't have. In the presence of that reality we can look across the street at the Jones's and not have to do anything in particular to be fulfilled. We don't have to keep up.

As we shift into the domain of being, we no longer have to do anything to be Whole or satisfied. It frees one up to do what is appropriate given the circumstance. It is what the Buddhists call 'right action'.

LESSON—LOVE

Sit quietly and breathe in, breathe out. Concentrate on just breathing until you begin to relax. Breathe in. Breathe out. Breathe in. Breathe out. Focus your attention on the energy center at your heart chakra. This chakra connects you to Love. It is the center of self-acceptance. Picture the color green, which is the color associated with the vibrational frequency of the chakra, emanating out from your heart in energetic waves.

Sit with the energy until you can feel it. Within this chakra of self-acceptance, know that your heart connection is always open and available. Know that you are enough, right now in this moment and at One with Love. Sit quietly and let the green energetic light and the word 'Love' penetrate your awareness.

MYTH #5—THE ONE-RIGHT-WAY

THROAT CHAKRA—SELF-EXPRESSION—*Pitfall: Lies (Shows up often as Righteousness)*

Where does the idea of one right way come from? It's part of our evolution. We have it time-stamped in our DNA and it is a direct descendant of separation. It goes back to a basic survival of the fittest when failure to survive meant physical death. If you didn't bag the beast or if you were bagged by the beast, you were eliminated from the game. Back in those times, when someone made a mistake it was most often fatal. Even a broken leg, a cut or scratch, a sprained ankle could and most likely would result in death. The imperative was to eat or be eaten and we didn't have much time to analyze which side the opponent was on. Quick, decisive, definitive. . .or we were dead. The one-right-way back then was the method, behavior and actions that would keep us from harm. It became so ingrained and predictable a way of behaving that it was invisible. It was just the way things were done.

Over the years the one-right-way has evolved from primarily physical attributes to include mental and emotional as well. We are taught at home and at school to have the right answer, to not make mistakes, and that it is not okay to be wrong. Being wrong threatens our survival on an emotional level. The social repercussions are damaging. No one wants to be ostracized, seen as stupid, or rejected from the group, basically, to be wrong.

Not only has our understanding of the one-right-way

evolved, our killer instinct has evolved too. Most of the time now, instead of throwing a spear at each other, we throw words. Through manipulation and coercion, our words demand conformity to our one-right-way. When it becomes obvious that we cannot convert another to the one-right-way, our point of view or opinion, then we must annihilate them. We do this through humiliation, derision, and rejection. These words are as hurtful as the physical pain of the tiger's tooth and in some ways they are much worse. The results last much longer. At least with the tiger, it is over quickly.

Life and living have evolved to being about looking right, sounding right, doing the right thing, having the right things, speaking the politically correct way, being associated with the right people—essentially making the right decisions in order to get the right result.

We want to be liked. We want to be included. This is not bad, but we so want to be good and to have the right answer, that our wanting so desperately to be that good person clouds our ability to be authentic. We will avoid embarrassment, shame and humiliation, being teased and made fun of at all costs. By defending our point of view, we alienate ourselves from others and we end up feeling alone, rejected, unappreciated, unheard, upset and hurt.

Gayle and I had an ongoing free-will versus predetermination (destiny) discussion during our first year writing the book. It was one of life's questions we didn't agree on. One day we were working and one of us said something that started the conversation all over again. I asked Gayle to explain her thinking. She did and made a rather definitive statement. I wish I could remember our exact words. It was a lively discussion. They always were. I started asking questions to try to understand her point of view and she got defensive. The more questions I asked (and I can be rather persistent) the more intense the conversation became. I had my questions and she had this point of view she was defending. The discussion took up most of the afternoon. We both knew we weren't going to resolve it—the mystics had been attempting to do that since the beginning of time—so we certainly weren't going to solve it that afternoon. When we talked about it later, we realized that two things had happened. After she explained her thoughts, she felt the need to defend her words even though she wasn't 100% committed to them. They were just her current thinking not the last word, but they had come out of her mouth and something in her felt she was on the line for what she had said. I realized that I had been so persistent with my questions because I thought maybe I was missing something. I wanted to understand what she was saying and what she really believed. She and I think alike and I value her ideas and thoughts. I really wanted to understand. What it looked like to our friend observing was two people arguing and both believing they were right. Madren C.

Following the one-right-way is very expensive in terms of conformity, loss of creativity, and unwillingness to see any solutions beyond our current truth. It creates in us an inability to act on a deeper sense of knowing. It also creates tremendous stress and confusion when we remain stuck in our righteousness even while it causes suffering. Separation is the price of the one-right-way. The payoff is that we still get to be right—right and alone.

We have discussions with people and before we know it, it has turned into an argument and we don't know why. In order to explain the argument, we sometimes fool ourselves saying we are playing the devil's advocate or some other role. As our point of view is challenged, the conversation heats up. The point of view may not even be what we really believe, but as we speak, the words become something we must defend. We have spoken them; we own them; they are now a part of us. If they are wrong, then we are wrong. Quick, decisive, definitive. . .Before we know it, we become very passionate about our newly developed point of view—our side of the conversation—to the degree that we stop listening to others while they are speaking, so we can plan what we will say next to convince them to agree with us, because of our need to be right.

Being right creates a fixed position in time and space, taking us out of the moment by locking us into a mental dialog whose sole purpose is to maintain the position. Only aligned positions, those in agreement, are acceptable; all others are deemed in opposition and unacceptable.

On one level or another, this myth is a part of every culture. Laws and rules are a natural outgrowth of the one-right-way. They are designed to ensure conformity to a certain set of standards, the culture's status quo. We are told these standards are in our own best interest. The degree to which we conform and choose to obey these rules and laws is dependent on how closely they align with our version of the one-right-way.

Within this myth, the means that are necessary to maintain the cultural status quo are justified. The end result is also predictable. Our adherence to our one-right-way reinforces separation and ultimately generates the isolation we so anxiously seek to avoid.

Here is what the little voice in our head might be saying: Boy, I'd better come up with the right answer. How dare you question me. Whatever I need to do is worth it. If you don't agree with me, I don't need you. . . I'm out of here. I don't want to try; I might do it wrong. If I try it, I may look foolish. I can't change; this is just who I am (how I do things or how I've always been).

LESSON—MY WAY OR...

<u>Purpose:</u> To bring awareness to how the myth—The One-Right-Way—determines your behavior and to shed light on all the ways that you are 'right' in your life.

<u>Instructions:</u> For the next three days, carry your journal with you and write down your one-right-ways as they occur.

HELPFUL HINT

Your one-right-ways are your version of how the world 'should' operate. Anytime the word should or shouldn't appears it is a clue that you are creating your right way. That guy shouldn't have. . .This should be. . . I should have. . .

<u>Instructions:</u> Write down your answers to the following questions:

1. Besides my partner, parent or spiritual adviser is there any one more right than I am? ☺
2. What do I gain by being right?
3. Why is it so uncomfortable to be wrong?

REALITY #5—THERE ARE MANY WAYS, MANY PATHS

THE THROAT CHAKRA—SELF-EXPRESSION—*Goals: Clear Communication, Creativity, Resonance*

We are so busy protecting and defending ourselves that we miss the opportunity to learn and grow. With every argument we have a choice. We can stay stuck in the myth, which predictably results in unhappiness and dissatisfaction, or choose to honor different viewpoints and experience being included, informed, and invested in unity.

There are numerous, incomprehensible options available with a multitude of shades to each option. As the mystics say, there are many rivers all of which lead to the ocean. The range of options and possible opinions are constantly being filtered by each individual's programming and experience, experiences that are in constant flux. What we believe to be true today may be proven to be inaccurate tomorrow. Science is constantly revising and changing what it believes to be truth; for example, prior to 1969 we didn't believe that a walk on the moon was possible. It was the stuff of science fiction. If we look closely at our own lives, we may see that what we thought to be true in the past in many cases no longer applies.

When we move from tying our value and worth to a particular point of view, we can be open to including alternate possibilities. We can move beyond what we currently hold as truth. But, as long as we tie our self worth to our specific opinions and beliefs we lock ourselves into place, unable to flow with the ever changing and evolving world. The more crystallized we become in that rightness, the more difficult it is to break out of the prison that we have created for ourselves, our crystalline shell.

We were working on the book and I found myself getting agitated. It was one of those days where we didn't feel quite in sync with each other or at least I didn't feel in sync with them. Finally I said, "I'm not feeling heard," and Madren said, "I'm listening to you. Isn't this what you just said?" I responded "Yes, but you don't get it." In that moment I saw a cascade of thoughts. My "I'm not feeling heard," wasn't that at all. That was just my way of not saying what I was really experiencing. It was, "You aren't listening to me," and then it became, "If you were really listening to me, you would see it my way and agree with me." Wow! What an epiphany. There were so many layers to get to the bottom and

I still hadn't hit bottom. The bottom was my own sense of worth. If there hadn't been a feeling of inadequacy, I wouldn't have been bothered if someone disagreed with me. When I saw that, I could let go of needing to be right—at least in that moment. Gayle G.

Each religion has its path to arrive at essentially the same place. Whether a path resonates with an individual is dependent on programming and experience. If we were born in Iraq chances are good that we were raised Muslim. If we were born in Italy, predictably, we were raised Catholic. The sheer location of our birth is often a determining factor in which path we walk. What we see as our right way is culturally, geographically, economically and temporally dependent. No matter what circumstances we are born into, there is a pathway presented and there are as many pathways as there are circumstances. For each group of people that follow their right way there is another group of people following another right way that works for them. There are always a myriad of tunnel-vision right ways coexisting in each moment. They are all valid whether you choose them or not. They are all different possibilities producing a desired result. This is true whether we are talking about religion, politics, economics, fashion or the color of paint for the room.

The point is to choose one that resonates and works for each of us. As we open to the multiplicity of paths, we have the opportunity to explore and experiment with paths previously closed to us, paths that have made others' hearts sing. What is required is a shift in perception, honoring and recognizing the validity of all paths, allowing them to coexist peacefully.

The first step is a willingness to acknowledge another's path. The next step is to open to the possibility that another's path may be as valid as ours. The last step is taking the action of honoring other paths as having validity equal to our own. It is a tall order but the bottom line is—this is possible when we let go of the idea that any one point of view has any more validity than another. As we let go of our rightness, the edges of separation soften and we can glimpse Oneness.

LESSON—OPEN

Sit quietly and breathe in, breathe out. Concentrate on just breathing until you begin to relax. Breathe in. Breathe out. Breathe in. Breathe out. Focus your attention on the energy center at your throat chakra. This chakra connects you to clear speaking, clear communication. It is the center of self-expression. Picture the color blue, which is the color associated with the vibrational frequency of the chakra, emanating out from your throat in energetic waves.

Blue Light   **Throat**

Sit with the energy until you can feel it. Know that who you are naturally acknowledges and affirms another's path, bringing all into the domain of inclusion and that honoring and including another is the highest form of Self-expression. Sit quietly and let the blue energetic light and the word 'Open' penetrate your awareness.

Myth #6—We Know What Is Real

Third Eye Chakra—Self-Reflection—*Pitfall: Illusion*

> Nothing I see is real. Everything I see is illusion.
>
> A Course In Miracles

There are many internal influences that determine our viewpoints and beliefs regarding reality. These influences begin early in our development and continue to shift and expand as we accumulate life experiences. For the first eight to nine months as infants we are passive observers, assimilating our world. When we begin crawling and experiencing our world on our own what we include in our world expands. As we begin using the physical form for mobility, we become aware of ourselves as a body. Because we see ourselves as bodies, we readily believe those things we can verify with our senses. If we can feel it, touch it, taste it, see it, or hear it, it is real. As small children we are also aware of the reality of a sixth sense, but as we age we are taught not to trust that sense. We are told that it doesn't exist. Even so and amidst this conditioning, our sixth sense occasionally informs us that what we are being told is wrong, that we are missing something.

At a young age our parents give us most of our beliefs. These inherited beliefs have been passed from generation to generation and determine what we view as real. When our parents said, "Don't touch the stove. It's hot and you'll get burned," most of us didn't have to touch the stove to take that as reality. Some of us accepted the belief without proof; others needed to test the theory. When our parents said, "Don't do that; God will punish you," we may have accepted this as reality as well without testing it. With this parental and cultural programming, what some call our domestication process, we began adding beliefs that are given to us and outside of our personal experience.

As our capacity to reason increased we began to think about our world and how we fit into it, taking in more information through personal experience, interaction with peers, books, and other outside influences. We decided for ourselves what our new beliefs would be and they became our new reality. Even though we were making decisions on a conscious level our previous programming continued to operate subconsciously. Much of our belief system was already in place.

Many events in history have influenced what we see as real. Prior to the advent of modern religion, nature and spirituality were deeply connected and perceived as equally real; they were the science of the day—the belief in how things worked and how humans should interact in their world. Plants and animals had a spiritual value that was honored. People saw their interconnectedness with all of nature.

With the increasing influence of religious doctrine the church became the new authority and determined appropriate relatedness between man, himself, and his environment but, around the 17th Century, a splintering took place between science and religion that further pushed the boundaries of what was defined as real. The work of Sir Francis Bacon, Sir Isaac Newton, and Rene Descartes set a scientific revolution in motion that further moved us from a natural, animistic world to a mechanical, mathematical one and we began to regard plants and animals mechanically, viewing them only for what they could provide rather than as having any intrinsic value. Once again, belief had shifted.

Our new belief in organized empirical research relegated religion, as well as spirituality, to the unproven. Tested and proven scientific theories created a new reality that governed the universe. These new theories were set in stone. Scientists knew what was real. They were the new experts. We listened to them and believed what they said, regardless of the fact that some observable reality, like gravity for instance, did not fit within their new scientific laws and understanding. The laws held tight though, until the 1920's when Einstein discovered the Theory of Relativity and set in motion another scientific revolution. (Interesting note: Now scientists are telling us that we are One and we refuse to believe them.)

The advent of mass media and current digital technology has added another dimension to our perceived reality. We watched the twin towers fall to the ground on television and felt the shock and fear—we were there. We saw the Pope elected from Vatican Square on television and felt the joy and excitement—we were there. However, when we saw the young boy, shot by the drug dealer on a crime drama, and looked on as the blood spilled from his chest—we were there, but that wasn't real. It didn't affect us. . .did it?

It had to be sometime between my 7th and 10th year. I watched a television program that was either Outer Limits or The

Alfred Hitchcock Hour. The show took place in an art gallery. The night security guard walked into the art gallery and turned to his right. I can't remember if he saw the painting or not, but I saw him looking in the direction of a painting, and then the reflection of light off a metal blade flashing through the air. The next morning the guard was found dead on the floor of the gallery, all slashed up. The painting on the wall in front of him was of a skeleton with a red and black cape draping his shoulders, holding a silver saber. At this point in the movie, I didn't know who killed the guard. For the rest of the movie when someone entered the gallery in the evening, they ended up in a slashed pile on the floor. At the end of the movie, the investigator went into the room at night and saw the painting. The skeleton stepped out of the painting, slashed the investigator, and stepped back into the picture with blood dripping off his saber. That night I went to sleep and woke up screaming, afraid that the skeleton was coming after me and would slash me up too. My decision: I am never safe at night; I never know who or what is going to get me. I need to learn to run fast. I should avoid pictures of skeletons; and at all cost, avoid art galleries. They are certainly dangerous places. Madren C.

The fact that we can see and hear real time news and view all the available programming on television would be unbelievable to past generations. If they could stand in front of our TV sets for a moment they wouldn't be able to discern what was real from what wasn't, but we are discriminating enough to know, aren't we?

I was in bed the other night and I woke up feeling very anxious. My body was tense and it felt like I was having a reaction to something very scary. I hadn't gone to bed afraid but here I was scared awake. As I allowed myself to stay with the feeling I flashed on a scene from one of the Star Trek movies, the scene where the bad guy was putting an entity into the ear of one of the good guys. It was a very pain-filled scene. Many scenes later the entity emerged and the good guy survived only to be told that the bug-like creature had laid thousands of eggs in his brain. Shiver. That was the shiver that woke me up. I saw that movie ten or fifteen years ago. I honestly didn't realize that it was stuck in my memory. I hadn't consciously thought of it since the day I saw the movie. Gayle G.

We watch movies—especially scary movies—and our pulses race and we may even cover our eyes because it seems too real. As we walk out of the movie we may still be agitated so we change our focus to forget what we have seen. Days, maybe years later, we have a dream, seemingly out of nowhere, and that same fear that disturbed us at the movie awakens us. Even awake, until we regain our senses, the fear remains until we tuck the scary thoughts and emotions neatly into a box—yes, it was a dream—thank goodness it's not real. We know what is real and what's not.

When I was a single Mom I used to watch crime dramas at night and many of the programs were about women being brutalized—a woman being raped, robbed, or tormented in one way or another. After awhile I began hearing noises and started worrying about who was outside. I wasn't sure if we were safe or not. It was just my small son and me alone at home, so eventually I had to turn off the television because I was scared and the programs just made it worse. I still don't watch crime shows today. Karen J.

Here's what the little voice in our head might be saying: I know what's real. Nobody has to tell me what's real. I trust my senses; if I can't trust them, what can I trust? Why would I consider any other alternative? That metaphysical stuff is new age garbage. I don't care what the quantum scientists are saying; I know what is real.

LESSON—TWILIGHT ZONE

<u>Purpose:</u> To bring awareness to how the myth—We Know What is Real—determines what you see as real and ultimately, your reality.

<u>Instructions:</u> Prepare to write your answers to the following questions:

1. What's real for me?
2. How do I determine what is real?
3. How can reality be different for different people?

REALITY #6—WE CAN DISCERN REALITY WITH PRACTICE

THE THIRD EYE CHAKRA—SELF-REFLECTION—*Goals: Clear Seeing, Imagination, Intuition, Accurate Interpretation*

We are all aware that there are the things we know and there are the things we don't know. We may know a lot about science and know that we don't know much about literature. There is another domain, not commonly recognized, the domain of what we don't know that we don't know. This is the domain of possibility. By talking about this domain we create a new reference point that allows us to be open to new possibilities of reality. Because it is deemed wrong to not know, we pretend to know. It is like the story of the emperor's new clothes or the time when the world was flat.

Come on. Who's going to tell
the little guy he's naked!

In the fairy tale, people agreed that the emperor's clothes were beautiful, because they were afraid. With their limited knowledge, 15th Century people agreed that the world ended at the horizon. Both were reality, for that moment in time, because of agreement. Were the emperor's clothes beautiful? No. He was quite naked. Was the world really flat? No. Columbus survived and didn't fall off the edge of the world. Fact or fiction, for both the fairy tale characters and the people living at the time of Columbus, it was their reality.

Man has made agreements from the beginning of time. Humans are hardwired to think, reason, and make decisions. Decisions are agreements we make with others and ourselves. By the very fact that we are human, we live our lives by agreement. We have inherited our agreements and they continue to accumulate as we experience life. These agreements have created our reality.

Through questioning, exploration, and experience, our understanding shifts to create a new reality. Reality is changing all the time. We don't live as if reality is constantly shifting, always dynamic, but it is.

Karen came in after lunch and I noticed that she didn't appear to be as present as she was prior to lunch. She was quiet and it appeared that she wasn't making eye contact with either Gayle or me. The loop my mind played was that there was something wrong and it went first to something wrong with me—perhaps she had an issue or problem with me and was avoiding being with me. Since nothing had shifted for me since lunch, my mind then went on to something wrong with Karen—when she returned from lunch, she was behaving very differently than she had been prior to lunch so I assumed something had shifted for her. My mind then began developing the 'something wrong with her' story. My mind began creating myth-stories about what happened to her over lunch. Later that day, a kind of wondering or curious mode began playing and I started examining the variety of different scenarios regarding Karen, and became aware that all of them were invented from my past experiences in my own life. None of it had anything to do with her. At that moment I became aware of and responsible for all these myth-stories, all this reality that I create between my ears. What appeared to me as my friend not being fully present after lunch allowed me the opportunity to see this habit, or tape loop, of my mind. It became so clear. I realized that I create my own reality in my life. I have total responsibility. There is no 'other' outside of myself who is responsible. For each of us there is only our version of reality. Madren C.

We can expand our version of reality with practice. We become aware of a new possibility in the moment that it presents itself to us. In this moment we have a choice and no matter what we choose, our frame of reference is changed. We can never go back to not knowing that the new possibility exists. Through our interpretation of the circumstances placed in front of us, we create our own reality. As soon as we accept the possibility that something else may exist, we have expanded our current awareness, we have expanded our beliefs, and ultimately our reality.

The cycle looks like this: first we have an experience. This doesn't address whether or not the experience is positive or negative, that is not the point. What is important is that we are constantly experiencing. During the moment of experiencing, an emotion or a reaction of some sort happens. From that reaction thoughts are generated. We think about the experience and judge the event—good or bad, right or wrong. Based on the judgment we make a decision about the experience. That decision creates our new belief. We automatically act consistent with the belief we have just created. Through actions and interactions with others we create our experience of reality. The cycle continuously repeats itself. Based on this cycle, reality is different for each person.

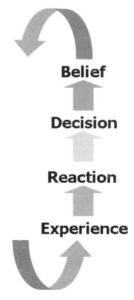

Belief

Decision

Reaction

Experience

We had been working on the book for six months when I left my consulting business. What I told myself was that I couldn't devote myself fully to the book with the distractions of the business. The reason I left was actually quite different. At the time I was doing quite a bit of work with another consulting firm. When I started working with this firm the owner and I seemed to click, almost as if we were long-lost sisters. As time passed, stressful times and tight money convinced me that I wasn't being valued. I didn't think the owner appreciated my contribution and I knew that she wasn't paying me as much as I was worth. Without open discussion, these feelings intensified month by month. I only attempted to have conversations about my concerns when it got to the point that I was about to boil over. Because I only halfheartedly attempted to clear the air, I never felt satisfied and comfortable with the outcomes. As we worked together I continued collecting evidence to support my point of view, totally unaware of what I was doing. Eventually, with little warning and without the honesty and straightforward discussion we had originally promised each other, I left. Through the process of exploring the myths, I came to understand that the conversations were actually unimportant. The owner would tell me that she valued my contribution and I couldn't hear her words because of my mind's story. It didn't matter what was said because I had already decided what she was thinking. I was making up the story of our relationship, both my part and hers, and acting consistent with it. I was making up the story within the context of my own beliefs. I knew that I was being abused. It fit with my own story of my self-worth. As long as I didn't believe in my worth, it had to follow that others would not see me as worthy. It didn't matter what was real for her. What was real for me was my mind's story, the story that I created all alone within my crystalline shell. Gayle G.

At the moment of experiencing we are aware only of the world as it occurs from our viewpoint. We don't consider that it may appear different for another. Only when we begin to have an awareness of more than just my world occurring, do we have the opportunity to include the possibility of concurrent realities. Once we are aware of the possibility that another's reality may be different from ours, we can choose to allow them their reality. In so doing we expand our own. This creates space for empathy and compassion for other viewpoints. This is the opportunity that we miss most of the time when we are in intimate or close relationships with another human being.

On the night I delivered my son, we were speeding to the hospital. It was midnight, dark, and we were on a two-lane road. Fortunately there wasn't a lot of traffic, but when we came upon a car, we passed them rather rapidly. We knew we had a good half hour drive to the hospital and the baby was coming fast. After we passed one particular vehicle, the driver sped up and started tailgating us, honking, flashing his headlights, and other rather obnoxious behavior. My mother-in-law was shouting, "Why is this jerk tailgating us?" This continued all the way to the hospital. When we pulled up to the emergency entrance he was still following us. When he saw me and my big belly, struggling to get out of the car and the attendants rushing from the hospital with the wheelchair, he must have finally figured out that this was an emergency situation. He turned around and sped off quickly. He must have been oblivious to the fact that we had turned into the hospital because he hadn't stopped. Now he could have been our guardian angel escorting us to safety but we didn't think so. Our interpretation of his actions was a little different. All he did was make us very nervous. More than likely, he had a different story as to why our car was speeding down a windy road in the middle of the night. His actions were consistent with his belief about what he had observed, which had created his reality. We were all making up our stories and acting consistent with them. Karen J.

So what is real? We've all had experiences that we just can't explain—a sense of agelessness, deja'vu, synchronicity, being in the zone, having the sense of really knowing someone that we have just met—and yet we've HAD these experiences. Since we can't explain them are they just imagination? We know they exist, we just don't know how to explain them. Are they real? Do we know what is real?

Perhaps we should rethink our agreements because watching fearful things does increase our level of fear. The mind can differentiate between what it sees on television and what is reality in time and space, but it still affects us as if what we saw was real. Telling a child that something they are watching on TV or that the story they are listening to is just make-believe does not stop the effects of fear or love from imprinting their psyche. Reviewing something in your mind creates the same benefit as actually and literally doing it. This technique is called visualization. There are many case studies of prisoners of war, concert musicians, and professional athletes from all sports using visualization to their advantage. There is a lot going on under the surface of what appears to be real. Perhaps we should consider looking a little closer at what we believe to be real.

> In his own work on quantum physics at MIT, Ed Mitchell had learned that at the subatomic level, the Newtonian, or classical view—that everything works in a comfortably predicable manner—had long been replaced by messier and indeterminate quantum theories, which suggest that the universe and the way it works are not quite as tidy as scientists used to think...Rather than a universe of static certainty, at the most fundamental level of matter, the world and its relationships were uncertain and unpredictable, a state of pure potential, of infinite possibility...Subatomic particles had no meaning in isolation, but could only be understood in their relationships. The world, at its most basic, existed as a complex web of interdependent relationships, forever indivisible.[8]
>
> Lynne McTaggart

What we have mentioned is only the tip of the iceberg. Every time we arrive at a new reference point, we think we have arrived at a place from which we can discern reality, but as time has proven, that point is constantly shifting. The pitfall is we think our reality is the only valid reality and that our most recent version is the final cut. It is a moving target. It is _so_ not stationary.

Not that long ago schools taught that atoms were made of three parts—neutrons, protons, and electrons. Now scientists have discovered that there are actually many more parts to the atom, so our reality has changed once again.

> In the 1960s, however, experiments began to show that protons and neutrons display internal structure and thus must be made of still smaller particles. Dubbed "quarks" by the American physicist Murray Gell-Mann after a line from James Joyce's

---

[8] Lynne McTaggart, *The Field*, HarperCollins Publishers, 2001

FINNEGAN'S WAKE, these particles come in six "flavors," called up, down, strange, charmed, top, and bottom. A proton consists of two up quarks and one down quark, while a neutron is made of two downs and one up. Combinations of quarks yield still more particles, although most are unstable and decay quickly to protons or neutrons. The very early universe was likely a dense soup of quarks and antiquarks.[9]

Stephen Hawking

Quantum science is really shaking up our current view of reality. All atoms are made of the same stuff. Molecules, made up of atoms, are obviously made up of the same stuff. Everything is made up of molecules and their associated atoms, so everything is the same stuff. Atoms are constantly in motion, so much motion that we exchange all the electrons in our bodies every few days. We could have electrons in our bodies today that were in Africa a week ago. If that isn't enough to make you question reality, respected scientists are also saying that our dream lives, our current personal lives, our past lives, our future lives, are all happening in different dimensions at the same time, holographically. This is what is referred to as parallel universes—the stuff of science fiction comic books. Some quantum scientists are also theorizing that there are an infinite number of parallel universes right at the tip of your nose.

Consider the possibility that what we have always held as reality is perhaps in fact illusion and that there is a reality that exists outside of the domain of our current experience. When we tap into this reality it creates a new possibility for living within a new depth of understanding.

---

[9] Stephen Hawking, PBS Online, Stephen Hawking's Universe, Strange Stuff Explained

LESSON—RELEASE

Sit quietly and breathe in, breathe out. Concentrate on just breathing until you begin to relax. Breathe in. Breathe out. Breathe in. Breathe out. Focus your attention on the energy center at your third eye chakra, located between your eyebrows. This chakra is your connection to intuition and imagination. It is the center of self-reflection. Picture the color indigo, which is the color associated with the vibrational frequency of the chakra, emanating out from your third eye in energetic waves.

Sit with the energy until you can feel it. Release the belief that you know what is real. Trust that in your letting go the answers will become available. These answers occur outside of your current intellectual comprehension and lie in 'Inner Knowing'. This inner knowing is what the mystics call universal knowledge. Sit quietly and let the indigo energetic light and the word 'Release' penetrate your awareness.

MYTH #7—THE ORIGINAL MYTH

CROWN CHAKRA—SELF-KNOWLEDGE—*Pitfall: Inability to Trust, Attachment*

> The greatest enemy of the truth is very often not the lie—
> deliberate, contrived and dishonest—but the myth—
> persistent, persuasive and unrealistic.
>
> John Fitzgerald Kennedy

One fundamental myth is the basis of all our stories and beliefs. It creates the context within which all these beliefs and stories play out. Most of us never question it. This is the myth that we are alone, that we are separate from Source, from each other, and from all of nature. This myth, what we call the original myth, generates the atmosphere of fear in which we live. This fear-based reality keeps us locked into habitual patterns that drive our behaviors and motivate our decisions and goals. This basic myth plays out in all areas of our lives. We see and feel its impact at home, at work, and in our communities. It is what allows us to see poverty, war, and the destruction of our planet and do nothing. It prevents us from being authentic which takes an immense toll on our happiness and sense of well-being.

I was working in Hawaii and got into a car accident. I knew that the accident meant that something was off in my life—I wasn't being present. My work in Hawaii wasn't the problem, so I went home to California to check in with my family. I had been married for three weeks. I asked my wife if there was anything she needed to tell me, because there was something off, and I instantly knew by her expression that this was going to hurt. In the year up to our marriage, she hadn't been faithful and had withheld and denied it. It devastated me and broke my heart. I didn't know what I could trust, obviously not myself and my own discernment, because I had totally missed it. I felt upset, hurt, angry, and isolated. It compounded the numbness that I was already feeling. Eighteen months earlier my mother had died of a terminal illness, and then three and one-half months after that, my father died in a tragic accident. I stayed in California in an attempt to reconcile with my wife, but found myself withdrawing further and further, not only from her, but from my business partners in Hawaii and from friends. I started feeling more and more separate and alone. My lack of communication with my business partners created even more separation and resulted in them excluding me from our business and any and all profits. To top it off, I had a falling out with my siblings about the same time. Not long after, I was in my garage looking for a tool I needed for the remodel that I was doing on our house and saw my climbing rope on the wall. I took the rope down from the wall, held it in my hands, looked up at the rafters and said, "This would not be difficult." I stood in the garage with my rope in my hands, feeling desperately separate, not only from all the people in my life, but from my own sense of self and any desire to remain on the planet. I was feeling too much pain and I had caused too much pain. I clearly saw how people can choose to end their lives. I don't know why I didn't do it—perhaps I owe my life to the fact that I paused for a moment. I put the climbing rope back on the wall and went upstairs to continue working, feeling very, very isolated.   Madren C.

The Original Myth

Ego

⇓
Separation
⇓
Fear
⇓
My Stories
⇓
Perceived Reality

The idea that we are separate and alone is the original myth. Belief in separation has a cascading effect. We see ourselves as separate and are immediately alone.   Our aloneness automatically presents fear. From that fear we create beliefs that in turn construct our reality—I am alone, not a part of the whole, and therefore I am vulnerable; if I am alone then I must protect myself. This need to protect ourselves, the result of our separation, creates a myriad of other false beliefs—our stories—that we have come to accept as true. This way of thinking becomes our unquestioned reality.

As we see ourselves as separate from the whole, the world is a scary place. From that scary place, the place of basic survival, fear is generated   the fear that there is not enough. Because we fear not having enough we see others as having power over us and that the power is outside of us. After all, if it were in our control we could make certain that we would always have enough. Because we cannot assure our survival, it becomes clear that we are not enough. If we were stronger, smarter, prettier. . .we might have stood a chance. In order to get enough we learn to play the game and our success depends on learning the way that successful others employ—the one-right-way. In this process of game playing, we learn to see the world as those we depend upon see it, and this limits us to believing that we know the difference between what is real and what isn't. Even if we suspect that we aren't getting the whole story, we dare not rock the boat. If we do, we might get thrown out. Our story is our proof—we are separate from God, others and ourselves. If we were 'One' with everything, surely we would be fearless and all-powerful.

The moment of separation occurred when were small children. At the point we realized attention had been diverted from us, and we were not getting what we wanted or needed, we felt hurt. We made an unconscious decision—this is bad— and our first resistance to life appeared. This resistance turned into a decision to do something different to remedy the current situation, beginning a pattern of behavior that was driven from our need for attention, validation, and love. It was self-perpetuating and solidified the decision that we were separate. When repeated throughout the next several months and years, the decision concretized into a certainty, rather than just mere feeling.

Our hurt and pain is translated into a belief that we are inadequate and unlovable. It feels bad to us, but we don't talk about it to anyone; it becomes our new point of view of how we must operate in our world. We feel hurt and unloved and quickly figure out that we must alter our behavior to minimize the hurt and pain. We can't be who we are naturally, so we must play act instead. We fine-tune our behavior, altering what we do, continuing to adjust to get more and more of what we think we want. Life becomes about finding the right formula. The motivator, the driver of our behavior, is getting what we want—and what we want is freedom from the pain. So we get really, really good at fine-tuning our behavior. We have to; at a very basic level we think our survival depends on it. We even say things like, "I'll just die if I don't _____." When we finally get what we want, we soon realize it wasn't what we were looking for, and we are off in search of the next great thing. The charade has begun.

Back in the 6th grade, not being left out of the in-group was important—very important to me. I was known for having great parties and was getting ready to have another as soon as school got out, celebrating our graduation into middle school. It was a boy-girl party and a friend and I had done all the planning. One of the popular girls came up to me and asked if my friend was coming to the party. When I said yes, she made me understand that if my friend was coming, the popular group wasn't. If I wanted them to come, I had to make certain that she didn't. I did what they wanted. I called my friend and uninvited her. I was willing to play their game in order to get what I wanted and I wanted to be included. Instead of inclusion I felt as alone as I ever had. That phone call haunted me for the next thirty years. At our twenty-five

*year reunion I apologized to my old friend. By the look on
her face, I knew that it had been a big deal to her too. No
apology could have ever been enough.   Gayle G.*

We become so accomplished at altering our behavior that
we forget who we are at the core. We forget what we were
really after when we started the charade. In fact, if asked, we
won't even remember that we were ever different. Instead of
being defined by who we are at the core, we have become
defined by the charade. We have forgotten what started the
game in the first place.

What we forgot we wanted, way back when, was love—
the compassion, the warm unconditional love and caring of
the family. The longing in our hearts is for this love, our
Wholeness. We learned to settle for what was available and
substituted something else for the love we needed. In the
process of settling, we built up our tolerance for pain. The
belief that we could be unloved was the initial inspiration for
the charade.

This myth is so ingrained in our reality that we believe
there is no other way. We don't even talk about it, let alone
talk about any alternatives.   It is just the way things are. As
we grow up, the separation story is naturally assumed to be
true, based on our own observations. We look out and see
another, separated from us by space, and know that yes, we
are indeed separate.

Our sense of separation is natural and predictable given
our current limited use of the internal software we've been
given. We are hardwired and come with a software package
from which we are selecting only basic functions of the avail-

able programming. It is kind of like having Microsoft Office on the computer and only using Word. Excel, Powerpoint and Outlook are just sitting there waiting to be discovered. We may not consciously know that the alternative programming is available, but something in us does. The longing in our hearts is an indicator that we know there is more. We just can't put our finger on it.

We hear a slightly different, yet similar story from many of our churches, a story that has filtered into our cultural identity. These religious interpretations tell us that at the level of our basic nature we are separate from God. In this story of separation, we are only human and God is outside of us. With that, not only are we separate from each other, we are also separate from God. Given the aloneness that this creates, it is no wonder that we may feel our very survival depends on our ability to be better, sharper, faster, or tougher than the other guy. For a large percentage of the world this interpretation is the accepted story—we are separate from God. This belief impacts us all.

The unquestioned belief in our separation supplies the cornerstone for the ideology that we are guilty of original sin (born sinners) and need to be forgiven. This tenet is the foundation for all guilt. Whether you believe in the traditional interpretation of original sin or not, society has incorporated it into its ideologies and it has been passed down to us in other shapes and forms. We may have heard the story as, "We aren't good enough as we are," or perhaps as, "Because we're not perfect we have to try harder." We may have also heard it as, "We are only human; what can you expect!"

If we take away the basic agreement, the idea that we are

separate from our Source, and replace it with Oneness, we see that what we really have is a case of mistaken identity. Original sin is the original myth. Before the original sin we were Oneness. After the original sin, we were separated from Oneness. The original sin is not some stain we were both with. It is our belief in separation. When we align with the reality of Oneness, what is there to be forgiven for?

Our misinterpretation of original sin colors our belief in the nature of mankind. We look at our world and see greed and selfishness. We see a lack of consideration for others. We see what appears as evil. Most of the time we aren't surprised; it's the nature of mankind. We look at ourselves, and if we are honest, see that we too, are capable of everything we attribute to those we perceive as outside of ourselves. It too, is the way we are.

MAY/JUNE 2005—NY TIMES HEADLINE NEWS
Military Details Koran Incidents At Base in Cuba...Kentucky Diocese to Set Up $120 Million for Abuse Victims...'No' votes in Europe Reflect Anger at National Leaders...Heart Device Sold Despite Flaw, Data Shows...Rights Group Defends Chastising of U.S...Russian Tycoon Given 9 Years on Tax Charge...Boarding Schools Rector, Under Fire, Will Step Down...Scrushy on Trial: Class, Race, and the Pursuit of Justice in Alabama...A Mini Enron on Every Corner?...

If we looked closely we might see our true humanity and know that we are actually One with everything. Then it would make it a little more uncomfortable to let children starve, to steal from each other, or to rape and pillage the planet. If we are One with everything that would mean that we are starving, that we are raping and pillaging ourselves. We can hang onto the myth of our separation, but. . .what if it isn't true? What if we really are One?

As you read this you may be thinking, "What do you mean, we are separate from Source! It's not a myth and I can prove it. We can't be 'Whole'. Wholeness would be pure and beautiful. If we are Whole, then humanity is in big trouble because our dark side is not very pretty. We've cheated; we've stolen; we've lied; we've broken all the commandments. And, even without our actions, our thoughts are not always pure. So, that's it. We must be separate. We can't be Whole if we've done those things." At least, that is what we've always been taught.

There is another aspect of the original myth. The mystics have called it 'fear of our own greatness'. It doesn't seem that way to us. Fear of our greatness! Not likely. What it looks and feels like to us is being totally separate—separate from our potential, separate from the greatness that we sense but cannot access. We all know that we are much more than what is showing up, perhaps not on a day-to-day basis, but at least in glimpses. Every one of us knows that. That is what stimulates our disappointment in ourselves when we don't participate as fully as we think we should. That is what makes us feel bad about ourselves when we are inauthentic. That is what moves us to try harder, to explore new ideas, to believe in a better life, and to search for what is true.

But, the resistance to our greatness is strong. It is easier to believe that we are separate; after all, haven't we proven that time and time again? Separation fits with everything we've been told and given the way we have been living our life, we can't see how we can realize greatness. Still, something inside knows we are much more and resists the idea of being separated from that. We become cynical or resigned when we feel helpless to reach our potential—the potential that we know exists. Cynicism and resignation are perfect examples of how we create separation ourselves.

Within the context of the original myth, which is the belief that we are separate—separate from God, separate from each other, separate from ourselves—we are pinned against the wall of our beliefs. These beliefs, whether ours or not, make up the invisible context within which we all live our lives.

LESSON—SEPARATION ANXIETY

<u>Purpose:</u> To bring awareness to how the Original Myth impacts your decisions and behavior and to understand how your experiences of feeling separate from your self, others and Source determines how you view your world.

<u>Instructions:</u> Answer the following questions in writing:

1. What memories do I have of being inauthentic or of not living up to what I see as my true self?

2. What memories do I have of being separate from others—times when I felt irrelevant, left out, or isolated?

3. How do I know that I am separate from Source? Can I recall any instances when I felt a sense of unity with Oneness?

REALITY #7—ONENESS

THE CROWN CHAKRA—SELF-KNOWLEDGE—*Goals: Wisdom, Consciousness, Awareness*

We could listen to mystics, scientists, poets, and various others, and we could look at the truth of our own experience. When we do we will find that our bodies are merely vehicles for experience. The reality is that we are spiritual beings having a physical experience. We have gotten mired in the physical experience, thinking that it is all that there is, and have forgotten the truth of our own divinity. By fully owning our physical experience while shifting our attention to what makes us feel connected and at home, paying attention to those things that matter deeply to us, we can make this truth a reality. We can become human beings rather than human doings. Imagine the implications.

> Man did not weave the web of life—he is merely a strand in it. Whatever he does to the web, he does to himself.
> Attributed to Chief Seattle of the Suquamish

> A substructure underpins the universe that is essentially a recording medium of everything, providing a means for everything to communicate with everything else. People are indivisible from their environment. Living consciousness is not an isolated entity. It increases order in the rest of the world. The consciousness of human beings has incredible powers, to heal ourselves, to heal the world—in a sense, to make it as we wish it to be.
> Lynne McTaggart, The Field

> The universe is represented in every one of its particles. Everything is made of one hidden stuff. The world globes itself

in a drop of dew...The true doctrine of omnipresence is that
God appears with all His parts in every moss and cobweb.
Ralph Waldo Emerson, "Compensation"

There is no life, truth, intelligence, nor substance in matter. All
is infinite Mind, and its manifestation, for God is All in All.
Mary Baker Eddy, Science and Health

The plurality that we perceive is only an appearance; it is not
real.
Erwin Schrödinger, Physicist

But if the great sun move not of himself; but is an errand-boy in
heaven; not one single star can revolve, but by some invisible
power; how then can this one small heart beat; this one small
brain think thoughts; unless God does that beating, does that
thinking, does that living, and not I.
Herman Melville, <u>Moby Dick</u>

Joy is the realization of the truth of oneness, the oneness of our
soul with the world and of the world-soul with the supreme
love.
Rabindranath Tagore, <u>Gitanjali</u>

Duality is an illusion based on perspective—there is subject
and object, separation. Without duality, all is one—the spiritual
light in me is the same as in you and in any other. The effect of
duality is the illusion that makes us feel separate from Spirit. It
is not Truth, but the Truth of Spiritual Unity cannot be seen
within the illusion of duality.
J. Michael Strange, <u>Common Spirit, Common Ground</u>

It is our denial of this Oneness that causes suffering. The
denial of this reality causes us to feel as if we are not enough,
to feel unloved, to feel as if we are missing something, to feel
that we are separate and alone. This denial creates the longing
because we know we are more. We spend our lives looking
for something or someone to complete us, and when we
succeed we will have discovered that we had it, that we were

it, all the time. We think we need love. In actuality, we are the love we long for. It is the cat chasing its tail; it's the grand cosmic joke.

> I was wandering like a lost sheep, searching outside of myself for that which was within. I ran through all the streets and squares of this great city, the world, searching for Thee, O God, and I found Thee not, because I sought Thee wrongly. Thou were within me and I sought Thee without.
>
> St. Augustine, <u>*Soliloquies*</u>

Although we experience separation from each other through the physical body, this body is actually our unique expression of Oneness. It is the vehicle for individual expression. Through our senses we are able to gather data and process it in accordance with our programming—our genetic patterns and life experiences. We have five commonly agreed upon senses—seeing, hearing, touching, tasting, and smelling. We have another sense, our sixth sense—or sense of knowing. Some describe this as intuition. We value the first five and largely dismiss the sixth. This devaluation of knowing is a prerequisite for the original myth. However, there is a mystical realm beyond the physical experience and our sixth sense, our inner knowingness, is our access to this realm. The five senses are a means to gather data, but we have another means, seldom acknowledged, available to us that is the link to Oneness.

There is a reason we have all six of these senses. On one level, our senses allow us to gather critical information about our environment to inform our decisions. This is the common every day experience or how we normally utilize our senses.

The vital purpose of our senses, one that we don't even recognize, is that they open the doorway, allowing us to be moved—by another's humanity, the ravages of war, the beauty of a sunset, nature's fury, a beautiful concerto, the hopelessness in a ghetto, a mother's love for her child. Being moved opens the doorway into our connectedness, our unity, the Oneness.

The door is not locked.

The doorway opens into the heart—our home. We know this is where we belong and we never want to leave. We have this inner knowing, our sixth sense, to remind us to be in union with the Oneness that we are, and then bring that into our day-to-day expression of our lives. It is our gift to each other and the planet. It is this knowing that propels us forward in our search for our authenticity.

As we allow ourselves to be moved, it is easier to access inner knowing or universal knowledge again and again, until

it becomes a natural expression of 'Who' we are. Our ability
to perceive this reality is like a muscle. For most of us this
ability has sat idle and needs a bit of exercise for proper
conditioning. Like building up our quads or biceps, this
may not happen overnight, but as you continually give
yourself permission to be moved and let life's circumstances
move you, you will continue to build the muscle that allows
you to stay connected to Oneness.

Another aspect of universal knowledge shows up in our
daily lives as unexplained coincidences. We may call them
weird, odd, lucky, or even accidental. We all experience the
extraordinary, although we may not always recognize it as
such. We don't always see the extraordinary in the ordinary.
Sometimes it can be scary when the unexplainable happens
so we blow it off, agreeing with ourselves that we made it up,
rather than taking the risk of looking closely to gain
understanding. We may even use terms like synchronicity
and intuition and not question the source of that knowledge.
They have become commonplace terms for what we used to
call coincidence. We are using these new words, but do we
really know what they represent?

We are talking about our Oneness, which when manifested
in concrete experience may seem mystical, magical or
unexplainable. We see Oneness naturally occurring in small
children before they have been taught to mistrust themselves.
Our experience of Oneness is just as valid a guide for us as
our five senses.

If ye do not recognize God, at least recognize His signs.[10]

Al-Hallaj

[10] Mansur Al-Hallaj was a 10th Century Persian mystic and teacher of Persian Sufism.

We spent a few days at Inei-Re, a retreat center, so that we could focus on writing the book. There was an enormous amount of dissonance and we kept pushing into the uncomfortable nature of the discussions. We were committed to honoring each other's speaking and point of view and when we had an insight we pushed until each of us had an awareness of the insight. A shift was taking place and we were unwilling to settle for less than full understanding. If you had been listening to our discussion you might have wondered about our process because we were very vocal and intense. To an onlooker it may have appeared as arguing. As we pushed into the difficulty of recreating the insight, the breakthrough was revealed. By trusting our inner knowing and allowing ourselves to stay true to our commitment in the face of discomfort, we found that it is possible for us to actually share in an experience or insight that one of us had. It was an intense and magical time. Madren C., Gayle G., Karen J.

As the intellect develops its understanding of the world through training and domestication, natural knowing diminishes in the shadow of the intellect's growth. We call it growth; it is more like 'un-growth'. As we empty of the belief that we have the answers, the natural answers, available to us as universal knowledge, begin to emerge. The more we empty, the greater the information available.

This is the mandate we are born into as human beings, that calls each one of us home. This mandate asks us to shift our priority from ego-centered existence to heart-centered awareness. This is the possibility to embrace our unity—our Oneness—and extend this Oneness to all beings. This is the opportunity to use fear as an awareness rather than as something to be avoided or denied. We can see the circumstances of everyday life as an opening to become aware of how our beliefs create our reality, and from that, our behavior.

THE CHOICE

Source	
Heart	**Ego**
⇓	⇓
Wholeness	**Separation**
⇓	⇓
Love	**Fear**
⇓	⇓
Awareness	**Myths**
⇓	⇓
Authentic Self	**Inauthentic Self**

This is the choice to use the moments that move us to shift from the unconscious acceptance of the myths into conscious awareness of Oneness. It is the Christ-consciousness, the Buddha nature, the Tao, the Ultimate Reality within each of us. It is the meaning of 'Namaste'—the God within me bows to the God within you. It is the path from the inauthentic self to authenticity.

LESSON—SURRENDER

Sit quietly and breathe in, breathe out. Concentrate on just breathing until you begin to relax. Breathe in. Breathe out. Breathe in. Breathe out. Focus your attention on the energy center at your crown chakra, located at the top of your head. This chakra is your connection to Source. It is the chakra of self-knowledge. Picture a pure violet light, which is the color of the vibrational frequency of the chakra, emanating out from your crown in energetic waves.

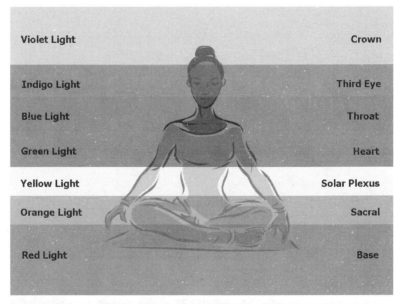

Violet Light	Crown
Indigo Light	Third Eye
Blue Light	Throat
Green Light	Heart
Yellow Light	Solar Plexus
Orange Light	Sacral
Red Light	Base

Sit with the energy until you can feel it. Within this chakra of self-knowledge, trust that you are One with everything. Surrender everything that you are, everything that you have built, to this Oneness. See that you are the creator of your life. Allow this new reality to grow within. Sit quietly and let the pure violet light and the word 'Surrender' penetrate your awareness.

THE EPIPHANY

I had credited God with creating a world of fear. Now I see that my world is my creation. I held God responsible for the folly of my own thoughts. And, I see that the world just 'is'—I give it meaning. I need only create my world through the lens of my commitment to find the answers to the longing in my heart and through them, the way from my mind into my heart.

I believed that God would create a world where there was not enough for all. Now I see that it was only my fear of personally not having enough that made me act in ways that denied God's abundance to all. I need only see my world through the lens of abundant potential to bring its fullness into reality.

I attributed power to those forces outside of me, to the gods of my mind, and denied the absolute power of Source. Now I see that I had given my true power away and with it responsibility for my self and for all life. The power is and has always been within me. I need only remind myself of those who have gone before me, and whose lives' paths were determined by their proclamation to stand for the divinity of all, to reclaim my power. This is my divine inheritance.

I lived with the sureness of my inadequacy, fearing I would never be enough, desperate to find approval from those to whom I gave my power, so that I could at last abandon my insufficiency and embrace the light of self-acceptance. Now I see that I was the one who betrayed my sense of self, and as I release my judgment I find Wholeness. I need only trust my heart in its pure knowing. It has been my constant companion, singing this song of Oneness and leading me home.

I asserted my right way, afraid to open to another's path, knowing that if I didn't get it right I would never be enough. Now I see that there are as many paths as there are human beings and that each person creates his own in his desire for fulfillment and joy. I need only embrace the diversity of this wondrous world to be expanded by the richness and complexity lying within the simplicity of the Whole.

I believed I knew what was real, trusting those to whom I gave my power, unwilling to step outside of my path of comfort, fearing failure and the sting of 'wrongness'. Now I see that I can perceive reality with practice and that my knowing prevented access to the unknown. I need only offer myself with an open and willing heart to see the truth of my divine interconnectedness with all creation.

Within the shadow and solidity of the myths, I had been certain of my separateness and acted in ways that prevented the emergence of the greater truth, the truth that would answer the longing in my heart. Now I see that I was the one who separated myself from Source and others, and yet in no way was I ever truly separate. Beneath the mantle of mind I was always and all ways One. I need only surrender to this reality to gaze with awe upon the Oneness in all things.

6
COMMITMENT AND
DECLARATION

Be the change you want to see in the world.
Gandhi

As we stand in what we already know is possible and reasonable, we ask ourselves the question, "What is it going to take to step into this arena that we know nothing about—an arena that we don't know, and yet now have glimpsed, and still be fully committed with every cell in our body, every ounce of the knowledge that we don't currently have, and stand for this unknown; this life, this world, this way to relate to people, this way to be with our children, that we can only yet dream of and is literally not known by us, that is hidden from us?" How can we support our Oneness? How can we let this not-knowing live in our cells? How can we have this be our new reality?   As we stand for Oneness, we reorient our genetics, our cells and our world view. This is the new beginning.

We have been creating our reality since we were born. We have come to a point where living by the myths hasn't produced the result we were after.   There is a possibility of being, outside of being at the effect of all the circumstances that we find ourselves in, as we go through life.   That possibility is created by standing for something—standing for something larger than ourselves, standing for something that moves or inspires us, standing for a possibility that is not yet in existence in our lives.

There are an infinite number of possible commitments to create in life, but only one that fills the longing in our hearts. We have the opportunity to choose a commitment that invites a future not currently present to become reality. That future is our passion. That future is our legacy for our children. That future is what we have always dreamed possible for ourselves and for our world. Actually, the use of the word *invite* is not exactly what we had in mind. The word that we were toying with may be more accurate, more powerful and determinant.   We are actually *commanding* the universe to align with our speaking. That is truly the power that lies in making a commitment and standing for something.

The point is that we are creating our commitments from nothing, through our speaking—by our declaration. At the moment of declaration our lives will now be driven and determined by that commitment and declaration, and no longer by beliefs of the past. In the domain of being, once we make the declaration, it is done; reality has shifted. Will we still have old beliefs and thoughts? Most likely, yes. The old thoughts and beliefs may occur from time to time, but we no longer need to be determined by them.

Empowered by our commitment, we will create beliefs, knowing they will determine actions and behaviors in support of our declarations. Instead of empowering the old thoughts and beliefs as we have done in the past, we now empower new thoughts and beliefs that align and support our new declaration. In the domain of doing, in how we navigate in the world, we will now have the opportunity to practice acting consistent with who we declare ourselves to be.

Where we are coming from makes the difference. Being aware of who we are being, while we are doing, creates the opportunity for transformation. We create who we are being by the very fact that we stand for something, rather than just reacting to the circumstances as they appear. This is the opportunity that is present when we declare ourselves. Once we make a commitment to who we want to be in our lives, we begin creating that reality. That commitment allows the action consistent with the commitment to transform our lives—to access possibility.

We cause the process to occur by being open, curious, and accepting. At the moment of declaration when we create this new reality, we shift the resonance field and create a new reference point in the field. This new reference point is then available for us and for all humanity from this point forward. What is now possible for us is available for others at the moment we cause and create that new resonance and vibrational frequency to be present.

> I believe this nation should commit itself to achieving the goal,
> before this decade is out, of landing a man on the Moon and
> returning him safely to Earth. No single space project in this
> period will be more impressive to mankind, or more important
> in the long-range exploration of space; and none will be so
> difficult or expensive to accomplish.
>
> John F. Kennedy

John F. Kennedy created a future by his declaration to send men to the moon. It was an unrecognizable and unpredictable future that his declaration made possible. His declaration created a future that no one could have predicted and that was previously inconceivable. That is what we create with the power of our speaking.

These experiences remind us that we are creators. With our commitment comes a passion to do whatever is appropriate to realize our vision, and with that passion we have the opportunity to see ourselves as creators, creating a future as did JFK, that currently may appear unachievable. With our commitment, our words and behaviors align with our stand.

The magic of being driven by our commitment is that with practice, our behaviors shift to be more in line with our commitment. With practice, our concerns shift to be more in line with our commitment. With practice, our listening shifts to be more in line with our commitment. With practice, our speaking shifts to be more in line with our commitment. The commitment becomes our new point of reference. The commitment becomes who we are, replacing who we previously considered ourselves to be. Our declarations verbalize our commitment and orient and propel our actions to be consistent with our commitment.

> Until one is committed there is hesitance, the chance to draw back, always ineffectiveness. Concerning all acts of initiative (and creation) there is one elementary truth, the ignorance of which kills countless ideas and splendid plans; that the moment one definitely commits oneself, then providence moves too. All sorts of things occur to help one that would otherwise never have occurred. A whole stream of events issues from the decision, raising in one's favor all the manner of unforeseen incidents and meetings and material assistance, which no man could have dreamt would have come his way. I have learned a deep respect for one of Goethe's couplets: Whatever you can do, or dream you can—begin it; boldness has a genius, power and magic in it.[1]
>
> W.H. Murray

In any experiment we begin with a hypothesis that we then test under different sets of circumstances by asking questions to discover if the hypothesis can withstand scrutiny. The grand experiment opens the possibility to create a new context in which we live our lives—one that is chosen consciously. The next step of this experiment is to set the context within which our declaration will stand. As we have moved through the myths and realities this contextual understanding becomes the natural outcome of awareness.

CONTEXT FOR THE STAND

In the past, we have considered ourselves to be our thoughts and beliefs, which created our identity and our

---

[1]W.H. Murray, 1951 Scottish Himalayan Expedition

experience.   We see that thoughts and beliefs occur and we choose which thoughts and beliefs to empower.   We have these thoughts independent of who we considered ourselves to be.   Therefore we now declare that these thoughts that occur and these beliefs that have influenced us are malleable, changeable and morph-able.   We no longer need to defend them.   They are not us.   They are just thoughts, beliefs, and habits that we have created.   We can un-create them in the same way we created them.   We are committed to using our lives as the laboratory to discover that we are not our thoughts and beliefs.   Who we are stands for this new reality, one where authenticity, intuition, honor and integrity are a natural experience.

INVENTING YOUR COMMITMENT

To be the most powerful, your commitment needs to come from your heart.   As you invent your commitment, your declaration will be a natural expression of the commitment. We invite you to search deeply and find what would answer the longing of your heart—nothing less can be your commitment.   It doesn't matter whether you fully believe in its reality.   Don't be reasonable.   Be unreasonable with yourself.   Allow yourself to be uncomfortable.   Experiment and create your own as your passion dictates.   We invite you to be committed to and stand for what moves you, what inspires you, what pulls you into life every morning.

OUR COMMITMENT:

To be an expression of Oneness

OUR DECLARATIONS:

Who I am is built by Love's expression. I am who LOVE is. Its expression shows up in kind and compassionate connections with all beings. Who I am is committed to being a clear and pure channel through which Source's gifts can be given to others. Who I am is committed to creating relationships founded on open and honest communication. Who I am supports, empowers, nurtures, heals and contributes to my life partner, my family, my friends, and all living things. Madren C.

Who I am is bowed in surrender. Who I am is 'One' with everything. I could call that by innumerable names but I choose to call that LOVE. Who I am is a loving, caring, and accepting wife and mother. Who I am is a true friend—willing to speak honestly and openly, while standing right in the middle of my fear. Who I am is a commitment to those I work with to meet them fully and allow the gifts to unfold. Who I am is an intersection for others with what is possible. Who I am is an opening into relationship and growth. Gayle G.

Who I am is Love and compassion for myself and others. Who I am is a caring, open, honest, wife, mother, sister, daughter, friend, co-worker. Who I am is One with All. Karen J.

LESSON—TAKING A STAND

Take a moment. Sit in silence and imagine a reality that answers the longing in your heart, a reality of Wholeness, a reality of love, a reality of heartfelt interactions.

1. Write down your commitment and verbalize your declaration.

BEING THE CAUSE

One of the outcomes of making a commitment and declaration is that behavior inconsistent with our declaration will now show up as an opening for awareness. When we stand for something out in the future that is not currently present we create a gap between our current reality and the future we are creating. The gap creates the space for those behaviors that previously would have been a problem, an issue, a concern, or a predicament to be used as opportunities for awareness. We are causing our thoughts, beliefs, actions and reactions to become our test lab for fine-tuning our behavior.

I was telling Gayle and Karen about when I was leading transformational courses in the woods. I was remembering those parts of the course when people shared about their intimate relationships, and in particular, about breakdowns in their relationships and lives. People would talk about affairs they had, cheating on their taxes, problems with their businesses and partners, and my job was to support them to find resolution and completion. I realized that I didn't have the experience to coach people in these positions. I hadn't had the experience in my life. I remember saying to myself, "I can't talk to people about affairs. I can't talk to people about how it feels to be betrayed. I can't do this with any integrity. How arrogant, standing here telling people, people who are open and vulnerable and raw, 'Just complete it; have the conversation. I will even coach you with what to say.' I've got to go out and gain some life experience...(boom)" and a big puzzle piece for my life fell into place and hit me on top of the head. At the time I was telling the story, I felt a physical jolt as did Gayle and Karen.

The realization I had was that over the last fifteen years I'd had a plethora of experiences, many extremely difficult and unpleasant, much of the time not understanding why they were happening, and that those experiences had been consistent with my unspoken and unconscious declaration to gain a variety of life experiences to allow me to do the work with people that I was committed to doing with integrity. Fifteen years prior in the moment that I said, "I am not experienced enough to coach people about this intimate stuff," I invited the universe to pour all these experiences into my lap. I called it into being. As the piece snapped into place there was no resistance to the idea that I had created it.

I completely owned my creation instantaneously. I couldn't be a victim about anything that had happened to me in my life during that time. I was the one that called it into presence. Madren C.

Living authentically will mean moment-by-moment alignment with who we say we are committed to being, by trim tabbing which thoughts and beliefs we choose to empower, and being consciously aware of our speaking and listening in each moment, to be consistent with the possibility created by our declaration.   All of life becomes the lesson inside the context of the grand experiment.

We now challenge ourselves, in each moment, to examine our thoughts and beliefs and to recognize when those beliefs limit our stand.   As we bring each fear-based belief into awareness it loses its power.   Seen as fear, it dissolves into the embrace of our commitment.   The power available to us when we invent our life authentically is that we are choosing to own and be responsible for the conditions and circumstances in which we find ourselves.   We choose behaviors consciously that will cause our commitments to be realized in the world.

In the 'domain of being', upon declaration, we become that which we have declared; we are the living statement of the declaration.   In the 'domain of doing', as we practice to align our behaviors with our new declaration, habits from the past, in the form of behaviors and beliefs will inform and influence the present.   We have spent years building our beliefs, and as with any habit, it may take time and continued awareness to become aware of and not determined by them.

Another level unearthed. Today Madren and I took the plunge. We were talking about what had kept us in a holding pattern on the book for the last five months. It wasn't our partner leaving. It was something else. As we talked, I felt the fear taking hold. I was afraid that I would allow old patterns to slip in and betray my commitment, that I wouldn't be able to trust my speaking, that I would stay silent and not speak my truth. Madren had suggested that the reason we felt stuck might have been because I needed to come to the place where I could fully partner, wholly owning my speaking and communication. Instantly, I felt the sting of "once again, my fault!" In that second I was out of Love, out of Oneness and into my mind. My mental dialog escalated as we talked, me attempting to explain what was going on, and he activated by my projections. His words were striking too close to home. I wanted to scream at him, to walk away from the book and our relationship. It was too difficult, too painful and yet, because of my commitment to Oneness, I stayed. After I had sat with the pain we began peeling away the layers. "What are you feeling? What is feeling threatened? Where's the fear?" I am afraid that I won't be able to honor my commitment to speak honestly—that the words will fail me, that I will fail myself and stay silent. "Go deeper." I have experienced trying to speak and feeling my throat constrict and the words just not coming out. When that happens, my stomach gets tight and I shut down. "Go deeper. What do you fear? Not being perfect?" No, I have never had trouble speaking when I'm facilitating workshops. I'm a great public speaker. "Go deeper. This is not business. This is talking about who you truly are, what you truly feel. Is more at stake?" As I talked I saw pictures of the child constructing the walls to create a safe space. I saw the immense importance she placed on being right and how that passed with her through the threshold of childhood into adult behavior. I saw the workaholic with the need to impress the boss and co-workers. I saw my interactions with friends and the subtle ways that I always made sure I was right. I saw my intolerance of anything that contradicted the world I had created. In those moments I clearly saw my fear. Since childhood I have built a tabernacle to being accurate, being right, on having the answer. I prided myself on my ability to get the answers first, beating everyone to the punch. I got the best grades and needed to be seen as the smartest. It was a competition with anyone who threatened my need to be right and to get there first. "Deeper. . .why was that necessary or important? Was it your way of elevating yourself to a position equal or better than those around you?" Let me look. The words came out quietly and very slow. I wasn't enough. I knew that I didn't measure up. Yes, it did make me feel more equal for a moment, but there was always the need to stay ahead, the fear that I wouldn't be able to. "Why did you need that?" I knew that I was not lovable, that something in me made people look at me with disapproval, with disagreement as to who I wanted and needed to see myself as being. I was unlovable and had to be seen as the smartest—right, in every way. That was the only way I would stand a chance of being loved. As I sat there with the rightness the pain was unbearable. It felt as if someone had thrust a knife into my heart and it was stuck there. If felt as if it would be there in my heart for eternity. I screamed out loud in the agony and tears began to roll down my face. Sobs shook my body.   I laughed despite the feeling of stuck-ness in my chest. Who would have guessed that my need to be right was so fierce and that my sense of not being enough ran so deep? Sitting right there with the pain was my only alternative. After a while it eased and lightness replaced the pain. I asked Madren, "Do you think we ever get to the bottom of our demons? Do we ever get to the point where there are no more to see?" We both laughed. Guess we'll find out. Gayle G.

We see our familiar beliefs and habits arising and may think our declaration is invalid—that we are still living in our old paradigm, not realizing that we are no longer who we were and in fact, would not be able to see the old habits and beliefs without the newly created reference point of our declaration. As behaviors and beliefs inconsistent with our declarations are presented, the opportunity is available to train the mind to shift how it operates to one of including all things in Oneness.

Oneness

Super Universe

Planet - Solar System - Local Universe

County - State - Region - Nation

Neighborhood -- Close Community

Close Friends -- Extended Family

Nuclear Family

Individual

We are constantly being informed by our level of awareness and beliefs. Our actions will correlate consistently. By attention and intention it is possible to expand that which informs us and naturally alter our behavior to one of inclusion. In fact, as a result of actions consistent with our declarations, expansion of that which informs us is a natural outcome. As we continue to expand our awareness every moment can become the conscious listening for Oneness.

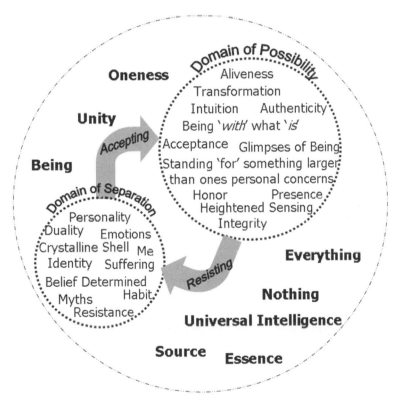

As we develop our awareness and become more awake we become present to new levels of consciousness. At our core, it is who we are. Consciousness is like a big circle that all else falls within, although this circle has no boundaries. Within this circle there is the 'me' we know—our identity—doing the dance of life.

The result of continuing to become more and more aware is that our caring and concern expands beyond our personal lives. Expanding our awareness opens the door to discovering our innocence, the innocence we were before we created our crystalline shells. It is a return to Oneness.

MEDITATION PRACTICE—ONENESS

May I be humble in my Love. May I bow to greet this day with gratefulness and delight. . .to arise as a flame of Love into the wonder of each moment. And may I stay present to this ALL DAY through.

Elle Collier Re

LOOK WITHIN

The meditation practice is a practice for life—The Grand Experiment. Supported and empowered by our commitments—what we stand for—the meditation practice facilitates quieting and calming the mind in a way that allows the discovery of our true nature and leads us into the full remembrance of who we truly are—Oneness.

Moving Energy

Moving energy is an intentional, focused and conscious process. Energy wants to move. It doesn't care how. Energy doesn't differentiate between happy or sad, anger or fear. It is just energy and it wants to move. As we go through the day we build up stores of energy as stress. Living in our worlds, as the energy builds up it gets more and more demanding over time, to the point that it prevents us from feeling. When it doesn't get moved, it creates blocks. The blocks create fatigue, a sense of impending explosion, and illness. The blocks keep us from being able to focus, from hearing clearly, and from being open to guidance. The first step in the process is to get the energy moving any way we can.

First thing in the morning or in the evening (perhaps both) go into a place that feels quiet and safe. Scan your body and see what you are feeling. Notice how the energy is moving and become aware of any places in the body that feel stuck.

If you feel nothing, choose to let yourself feel. Generate any emotion you choose to facilitate the movement of energy. Take deep breaths—in and out, in and out. If you find areas that are tight or stuck, direct your awareness to those areas and see what tension or emotion is being held there. Allow yourself to release it. Breathe into the stress or emotion and let it go completely. Jump up and down. Dance around and hoot and holler. Don't worry about how silly you may look. That is part of the process too. It helps us get over ourselves and gets the energy moving at the same time.

Sit and Be Still

This is your time to be calm, quiet, and still. It is a sacred part of the meditation. Sit and be still and surrender your previous ways of doing and being. Give it all back to Source. Be in the stillness until you become the stillness. Stillness does not mean that your mind *will* be silent; and yet, it may. It means that you will not engage in the dance of the mind.

Contemplate

Pick only one thought, belief, myth lesson or word

associated with a chakra. This could be something that has been in the background troubling or inviting you. This could be a belief or thought that you have observed and that is inconsistent with your declaration. It could be the nature of the universe or your place within it? It can literally be anything that appears to have importance to you.

Listen for Guidance

Ask questions. Inquire into the nature of the worry, the concern, the thought or belief. Find that place of neutrality, where you neither want nor need the answer to be anything specific, where you are truly interested and curious about the Truth and only the Truth. Sit quietly and listen for guidance.

Express Gratitude

Thank your self for your willingness to be right here in the middle of this process. Thank your Self (Source) for giving you the insights and information you were ready to hear in this moment. Express your willingness to listen whenever there is more to be given.

Move Forward

Realign, reintegrate, and re-embrace yourself in compassion and love. Be willing to dive deeper, deeper, deeper. . .further, further, further.

> The answer is, dig deeper; Find that fountain; find out where that joy is; find out where that love really is. When you dig deeply enough the fountain provides you all the magnificence of the divine.
>
> Elle Collier Re

7
JOURNEY TO
THE SUMMIT

Our grand experiment has taken us from the domain of cataleptic creation to the domain of conscious creation where possibility lives. On our journey along the steep mountainous slopes, we have stopped at the tea houses of myth and belief and discovered that there were limits to the nurturing available there. Oneness could only remain a myth itself as long as our view was obscured by the fog of fear. The fog overlaid our senses, clouding our self and world view. There was a limit to what we could see—a limit to what we could hear—a limit to what we could feel—a limit to what we could be.

We trekked deeper and deeper into the canyons of knowledge and up into the peaks of awareness at ever increasing elevations until we summited and caught a glimpse of the possibility of actually being something beyond whom we always considered ourselves to be—the radiant magnificence of being human, so far beyond our imaginings. It was a moment of awareness and we saw that we were the catalyst driving and causing our experience in the world.

The ecstasy of having achieved the summit was mixed with the wisdom that we can't bask in the moment of awareness at the top of the world for long, having gone further than we ever thought we could. There was further to go— always further. We must expand beyond the elation and relaxation of the summit—the realization that we are consciously creating our world—and exercise discipline and draw on our commitment to allow each step to be made consciously all the way Home.

What was ahead was the most dangerous part of the

journey. It would require a diligence and alertness that we hadn't yet experienced in our lives. Being completely challenged we now needed to draw on reserves we didn't know existed to step intentionally into our expanding awareness.

When we return to base camp, assuming we will, we will stand in the experience of going beyond what we ever thought possible, knowing who we discovered ourselves to be was the possibility of being One with everything—the Oneness we were looking for when we began our experiment—the longing of our hearts.

THE COSMIC JOKE

Fast forward. . .many mountains later. . .Looking back we laugh out loud—loudly—belly laugh loud—and realize that we didn't have to make the climbs after all. And then . . .laugh again. . .with the realization that it was perfect and each element of the experiment was absolutely necessary to get us to this point on the never-ending journey.

The joke is that we are creating all the time—we judge, we know, we have the one-right-way—but this is Source in man's image. It is why we act so strongly when we are thwarted, why we have to be right. We behave as if we are Source, although we would rarely acknowledge it. The Source we behave like is the Source of separation that we have invented. Separation is the same for all human beings. It's the overlay. It's our act. It's the charade we play. Our individual masks vary with our experiences of life and unique personalities, but we are Source, pretending not to be Source. **IT IS OUR BIGGEST ACT.**

THE DUALITY

The Source of Union, of Wholeness, of Oneness is the Source that invented man in his image. This is a Source of inclusion, the Source of all that is (physical, emotional and spiritual bodies), true authenticity free from the binds of any man-made rules and beliefs. This is the Source of Unconditional Love— total acceptance.

The Source of Separation is the Source that man invented in his image. This is a Source of rules, judgment, beliefs, righteousness, arrogance, taboos, exclusivity, isolation, the denunciation of ourselves as Source. This is the Source of fear— rejection.

In actuality—it is all Source. If Source exists, Source is everything; Source is all things.

Campbell, Gregory and Johnson

WHAT NOW?

To free ourselves completely from the cosmic joke we have to let go of *all our beliefs*. Once we have accepted the possibility of our Oneness the longing in our hearts will draw us ever forward. There is no going back now—only further, further, further. Now that we know what awaits us, nothing can stop our awakening to the reality of Oneness. Only our willingness and determination to dig deeply, until at last we reach the core of our beliefs and surrender our final protective armor, will allow us complete communion with Source.

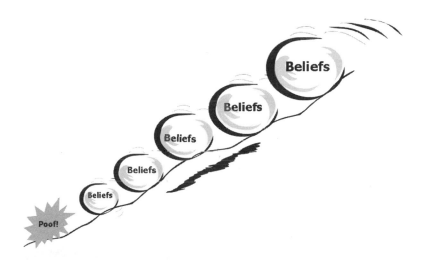

As we continue to practice the exercises found within the book the awareness will intensify, until in awe, we find that we have established a link to Source, and can then listen cleanly, without the need of any externally imposed structure.

How long will it take? That is a question that each one of us has to answer for ourselves. How determined are we?

How willing are we to dig into those places that hold our deepest pain? Can we sit in the midst of the ache and let it be?

Have patience. Expose one layer at a time. Let go of any expectation.   Continue to notice those things that catch you and spin your mind. Any time you react to something, to anything, see it as an opportunity for further surrender, and surrender this too. As you remain openly willing to let go of all that you have believed yourself to be, the closed doors swing open.

Where does Oneness live?   It lives beyond belief. . .and thus our journey continues.

PRACTICE!!! PRACTICE!!! PRACTICE!!!

ABOUT THE AUTHORS

MADREN CAMPBELL, a coach and consultant, works with individuals and businesses to see through their self-limiting beliefs. He also spends part of his time as an outdoor adventure guide where he uses exploration, ocean sailing and mountain climbing as a means for assisting others to transform their lives. Madren's commitment in life is to empower others to fulfill their life's vision and realize their magnificence. As a child Madren felt a strong connection with Jesus that, throughout the years, has only deepened. For the past twelve years he has studied with teachers of mystical Christianity and non-dualism. Previously, for three years he practiced Tibetan Buddhism and as a student of Shamanism, he participated in both South American and Native American vision quests.

GAYLE GREGORY left corporate America to realize her dream of sailing to Mexico in 1997. While there she spent many hours in contemplation and glimpsed the truth of the human condition. Since returning her complete focus has been on seeing her own fears, beliefs, ideas and concepts with absolute clarity, in order to be a clean, clear mirror for others to realize their own authentic nature. Her vision is to create a global community where people can feel safe enough to risk coming out of hiding to be who they really are. Raised in a protestant home, Gayle's spiritual path opened to embrace the diversity of teachings. She has studied Sufism, mystical Christianity, Advaita and briefly, Buddhism. It is through all these teachings that Gayle found her way back to relationship with Yeshua. She now views the Universe as her teacher, aware of the gifts of growth it constantly offers.

KAREN JOHNSON BROOKSHIER returned to the world of finance in August of 2005, midway through the book project. Her work life, which she calls her ministry, is based upon integrating love in the workplace, providing a blessing to humanity. Karen was raised in a Catholic home but realized early that some key pieces were missing from her spiritual education. With this realization Karen set in motion a spiritual journey of 20+ years that continues to this day. She has studied Christianity, Buddhism, Islam, and New Thought. Karen is currently on the Board of Directors of the Unity World Healing Center and the World Healing Institute, in Lake Oswego, Oregon.

Pure Possibility offers coaching and consulting for individuals and businesses desiring to see through their fears and radically alter their behaviors and outcomes.

You can contact the authors at:
Info@Pure-Possibility.org

or

Pure Possibility
2121 Reed Rd.
Hood River, Oregon 97031
503-313-1260

Also, please visit their website at
http://www.Pure-Possibility.org